JavaScript
Made Simple

P.K. McBride

MADE SIMPLE
BOOKS

Made Simple
An imprint of Butterworth-Heinemann
Linacre House, Jordan Hill, Oxford OX2 8DP
225 Wildwood Avenue, Woburn, MA 01801-2041
A division of Reed Educational and Professional Publishing Ltd

℞   A member of the Reed Elsevier plc group

OXFORD AUCKLAND BOSTON
JOHANNESBURG MELBOURNE NEW DELHI

First published 1997
Reprinted 1998, 1999, 2000 (twice)

TRADEMARKS/REGISTERED TRADEMARKS
Computer hardware and software brand names mentioned in this book are protected
by their respective trademarks and are acknowledged.

British Library Cataloguing in Publication Data
A catalogue record for this book is available from the British Library

ISBN 0 7506 3797 8

⚘ Typeset by P.K.McBride, Southampton

Archtype, Bash Casual, Cotswold and Gravity fonts from Advanced Graphics Ltd
Icons designed by Sarah Ward © 1994
Printed and bound in Great Britain by Scotprint

Contents

Preface

If you want to make your Web pages more active and interactive, you should be exploring JavaScript. As programming languages go, it is one of the easiest to learn. Though you can produce quite extensive applications with it if you really want, it is designed for small-scale work. Blocks of JavaScript code can be interwoven with standard HTML to add an extra dimension to your Web pages.

This book is not intended for proficient programmers who just need to pick up the rules and the vocabulary – there are plenty of other books already on the shelves that do that job. It is aimed at those people who have little or no prior experience of programming, and it starts from scratch. I have concentrated on the basic concepts and practical uses of the language, and tried to avoid getting bogged down in technicalities.

JavaScript Made Simple will take you through to the point where you can write small scripts to enhance and add interest to your Web pages. I hope it will also give you the foundations and the confidence to go further into the language. Each feature is demonstrated at work in a short example, as new concepts are best learnt through practical work. You will find exercises at the end of most chapters – use them to test your knowledge and to experiment with new ideas.

The text files for the larger examples, and for all of the answers to the exercises, can be found on the Made Simple Programming Web pages at the Butterworth-Heinemann site, at:

http://www.bh.com

P.K. McBride, September 1997

1 Introducing JavaScript

What is JavaScript?

JavaScript is the thing that will add some zing to your Web pages. It will give you action and interaction, make your readers respond better to your pages – and your pages respond to your readers!

JavaScript was developed by Netscape Corporation, specifically for use in the construction of Web pages. It is a programming language, but not one that can be used to create full-function stand-alone applications. It is designed to be used in conjunction with HTML – its code is intermingled with normal HTML code, and almost all of its interaction with the screen and the user is through HTML's facilities.

JavaScript shares some features with Java, but is significantly different in many ways – for a start it is far simpler!

This book does not assume that you know anything about Java or HTML, but does assume that you are familiar with Windows and Netscape Navigator.

What can you do with JavaScript?

Using JavaScript routines in your Web pages, you can:

● animate graphics and text – to a limited extent;

● play sounds;

● have better control of the display of windows and frames;

● check information entered into forms, and give your readers instant feedback.

LiveWire and LiveConnect

LiveWire JavaScript is a version of the language designed for use on Web servers – computers run by businesses and organisations to provide services to the World Wide Web.

LiveConnect enables you to link Java applets into JavaScript. You really need to be able to program in Java to make use of this.

JavaScript Made Simple is intended for non-programmers who want to learn enough of the language to improve their home pages. There isn't room here to cover either LiveWire or LiveConnect.

JavaScript in action

The best way to see JavaScript in action is to write the routines into your Web pages and view them in your browser – and there are plenty of examples in this book for you to try. But just to give you an idea of what it can do, here's a screenshot of JavaScript in action, and an outline of what has been going on.

The text, data entry areas and the button were created using standard HTML code. When the reader clicks the 'Get quote' button, a JavaScript routine is brought into play. It uses the 'Value of board' figure and the 'Home region' selection to calculate the cost of the insurance. This value is displayed in the 'Quotation' field, and a dialog box opens offering the reader a written quote. Clicking its 'OK' button starts a routine to get contact details from the reader and e-mail a quote. If 'HotWheels' was able to take credit card payments over the Internet, the system could go straight from on-screen quote to purchase.

Plain HTML will not give you this instant response and feedback. JavaScript will – and for remarkably little effort. There are fewer than a dozen short lines of code behind this screen.

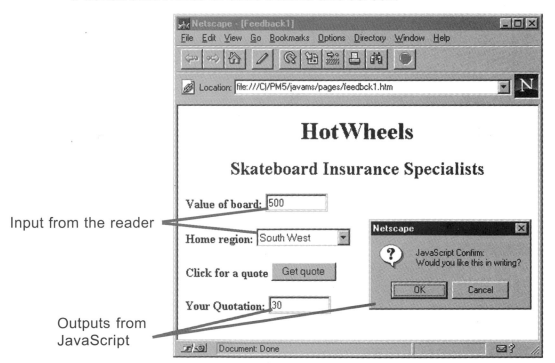

Input from the reader

Outputs from JavaScript

Programming languages

A computer can only understand one language, and that is *machine code*. This consists of (binary) numbers that the chip translates into instructions, values and memory addresses. The instructions are extremely simple; e.g. 'move this value into memory at this address'; 'compare these numbers'; 'increment this value'.

There was a time when people wrote programs in machine code, but no-one in their right mind does it now – it's very hard work and there are better ways to write software.

Most programming languages use words and structures that are (more or less) comprehensible to humans. The programmer writes sequences of instructions as a text file – known as the *source code* – which must then be converted into machine code for the computer. There are basically two ways of doing this.

● Some programming languages are *compiled*. The source code is passed to a *compiler* program, which first checks the text for syntax errors, and if it finds any, stops and displays a list of errors. The programmer must sort them all out and produce

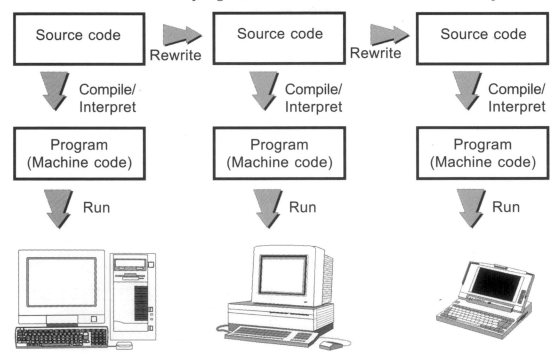

error-free code before the compiler will go on to the next stage and turn the text into an executable program. This is a block of machine code and can only be run on the right sort of machine – normally the same type that it was compiled on.

If you want to run the same program on different platforms, such as Windows PCs, OS/2 computers and Macintoshes, you can – in theory – take the source code across and recompile it. In practice, the code will normally need some rewriting because each machine tends to do some things in its own special ways.

● Source code can also be *interpreted*. Here, the code is processed by the *interpreter* during execution. Each line is taken in turn, checked for errors, then – if it's error-free – converted to machine code and executed. As with the compiled languages, you normally have to rewrite the source code to transfer a program to a different platform.

JavaScript is an interpreted language, but unusually – and happily for us – the same code will work on any type of computer, as long as it is running Netscape Navigator. The interpreter is built into Navigator, and it is Navigator that handles the differences between hardware platforms.

Take note

There are two versions of JavaScript and many versions of Netscape Navigator. Netscape 2.0 can handle JavaScript 1.0. Netscape 3.0 and later can handle JavaScript 1.1 (and 1.0). You cannot run JavaScript on earlier versions of Netscape. The latest version of Internet Explorer (4.0) can also handle JavaScript. See page 63 for more about writing pages to suit different browsers.

Programming with objects

You have probably heard of object oriented programming languages. Well, JavaScript is an object **based** language, which is similar, but not quite the same. All the major programming languages developed in the last few years are object oriented or object based, and the reason is simple – you can produce better, more reliable programs faster if you use objects.

Here's the major difference between a 'traditional' programming language and one based on objects. Think of a clickable button on a Form. If you wanted to create this in a traditional language, you would have to write some code to draw the button on the screen, then write some more to track the mouse movement (drawing the pointer) and watch for the click, and some more to draw the button as it is clicked, and then – at last – you can write the code to do the job called up by the click. Oh yes, and you'll have to do most of it again next time you want another clickable button!

JavaScript, like other object based languages, *knows* about buttons. It knows what they look like and how they interact with mice. If you want a button in JavaScript, all you have to do is pick up the button from your HTML code and specify what to do when it is clicked.

For instance, this single line of code creates a button and responds to a click:

```
<INPUT TYPE=button VALUE="Click Me" onClick="self.status='Thank you for clicking'">
```

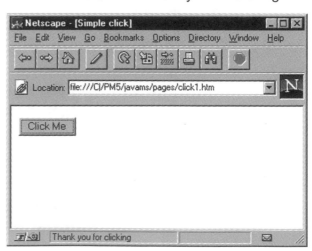

In this case, the JavaScript code simply writes a message in the status line. The important point here though, is how easy it is to create a button and respond to a click on it.

JavaScript objects

An object is a bundle of routines and values that define its appearance (if it is visible) and its interaction with other objects and the rest of the program.

Most JavaScript objects are visible parts of the HTML system – buttons and text areas, forms, frames, windows, even the page itself. Some objects are abstract, and are there to provide extra facilities to JavaScript. These include String (for holding text), Date (for finding and setting the time and date) and array (for managing groups of objects). There is also a Math object, which is essentially a collection of trigonometry and other mathematical functions and constants.

Whatever the type, all JavaScript objects have **properties**, most also have **methods** and **event handlers**.

- **Properties** define the object. Typical properties are width, height, colour, and status. All can be read and some of them changed by JavaScript code; some are determined by outside events, others can only be set within HTML.

- **Methods** are built-in routines which work normally on that object to which they belong. HTML objects, for example, have a **focus** method which brings them into focus – putting the cursor in a text field, highlighting a button, or making a frame active.

- **Event handlers** are routines that pick up actions that affect the object. Buttons, for instance, have an **onClick** event handler that knows when the reader has clicked it. Much of the JavaScript code that you write will start from one of these event handlers.

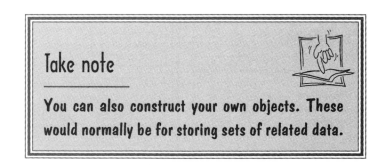

Take note

You can also construct your own objects. These would normally be for storing sets of related data.

Object names

If you need to read or set the properties or value of an element, or move to another frame or window, you must be able to identify it. There are two aspects to identifying an object in JavaScript – where the object fits into the scheme of things, and its given name, if any.

Objects exist in a hierarchy, with smaller ones contained within larger ones. A **window** has (optionally) **frames**, then a **document**. This may contain **forms** which hold **elements** such as **text inputs** and **buttons**. The document may also contain **images**, **targets** and other elements.

The larger objects – windows, frames, documents and forms – are automatically named as 'window', 'frame', 'document' and 'form'. You only need to use names if you have more than one of that type in the pages that are used by the *script* (JavaScript program).

Other objects need names if they are actively used by the script – you will come across examples of this later, particularly where we are working with Form elements and images.

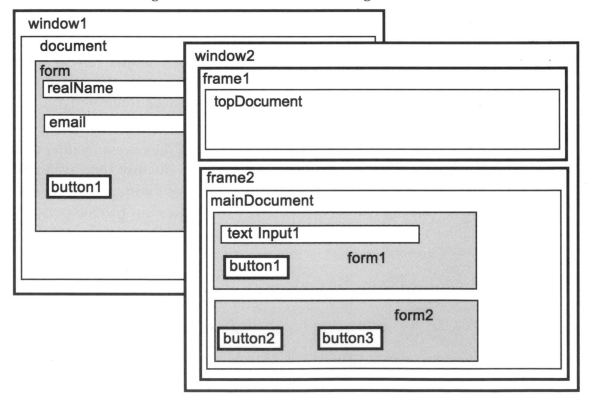

Rules for names

Names must be single words, must start with a letter and may contain any combination of letters, digits and the under_score.

● JavaScript is case-sensitive – upper and lower case characters are not the same. 'Button1', 'BUTTON1' and 'button1' are three different names.

You will make life easier for yourself if you keep names simple. Stick to lower-case letters, using capitals only where you have compound names, where capitals mark the start of each word. e.g. 'surname', 'price', 'address1', 'totalCost', 'mailToMe'.

With short scripts, you can get away with numbered names – 'button1', 'button2', etc. With longer ones, you should make your names more meaningful – 'startButton', 'stopButton' and the like.

Names and the hierarchy

Names must locate the object in its hierarchy. Suppose you had a script in the document in *window1*, in the example opposite. To refer to the *realName* text box, you would use *document.form.realName*. Note the full stops used to separate the parts of the name. If the object is in another window, the window name must also be included – *window2.frame2.mainDocument.form1.textInput1*. It can get a bit long-winded, but that's JavaScript!

Properties

In practice, most of the time you want to refer to a **property** of an object, rather than the object itself. Text boxes, for instance, have a Value property which is the text they contain. The property is added to the end of the name, so the *email* address, in *window1*, would be identified by *document.form.email.value*.

The links between objects in the hierarchy are actually properties. *button2* is a property of *form2*, which is itself a property of *mainDocument*. The property connection also works up the hierarchy. *form2* is a property (parent of) *button2*. This can be useful as you will see once we start getting into some real scripts.

9

Tools for the job

One of the good things about JavaScript is how easy it is to get started. The only tools that you need are Netscape (version 2.0 or later), a text editor and software for producing and editing images.

Netscape

Netscape serves two purposes. First, it is essential for running your programs – the JavaScript interpreter is built into its system. Second, there's a decent little HTML editor in the Gold versions of Netscape 2.0 and 3.0, and in Communicator, where it is called Composer.

It is not a brilliant editor, in any version (the differences between the Gold editor and Composer are insignificant), but it offers a quick and easy way to lay out pages. The toolbar has all the tools you need for formatting text and for inserting images, links and targets. It also handles tables quite efficiently.

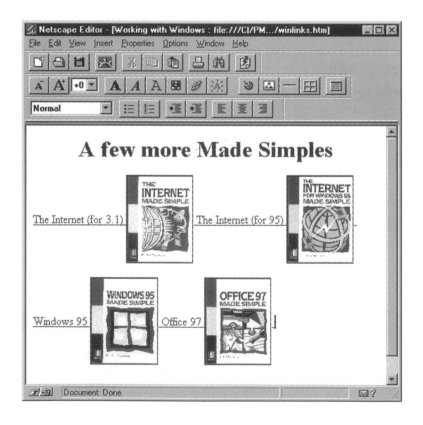

On the downside, the Netscape editors cannot cope with forms, or frames, which is a shame as some of the more interesting JavaScript uses revolve around these. And, of course, you cannot write JavaScript directly into the editor – well, Composer does have a little window for adding JavaScript to inserted images and links, but it is too small to be of much use.

The text editor

You can use your favourite word processor for editing the text, but it probably has far more facilities than you need. WordPad (Write in Windows 3.1) or NotePad will do the job nicely.

WordPad has a couple of advantages – you can reopen recently-used files from the list at the bottom of the File menu, and its Replace function is handy if you want to change every occurence of a name.

NotePad is smaller, quicker to load and it saves in Text format without being told. Try them both and see what you think.

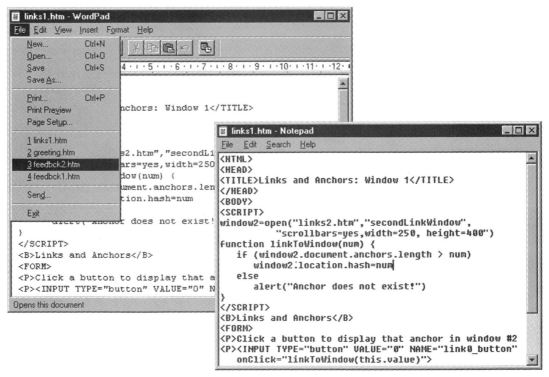

Graphics software

Web browsers are designed to handle images in the GIF and JPG formats. The standard Windows' Paint tools produce files only in BMP and PCX formats. If you want to create your own images for your pages – rather than just download other people's efforts from the Web – you must have suitable software.

One of the best packages around is Paint Shop Pro. It can convert existing images between almost every known format, but also has an excellent set of painting tools, plus some very sophisticated filtering and editing facilities, so that you can produce your own images. Despite the range and quality of its features, Paint Shop Pro is not difficult to use and it's cheap. Download an evaluation copy and try it for yourself!

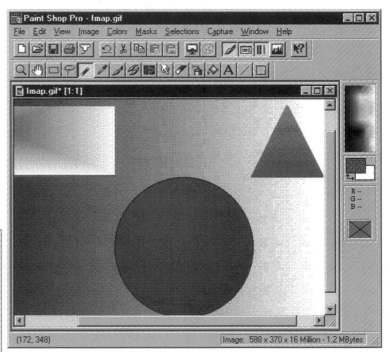

Paint Shop Pro is being used here to produce the image map for the example in Chapter 7. The shapes are very simple – but the shading effects are complex.

Tip

You can find out more about Paint Shop Pro and download a copy from the developer's Web site at:

http://www.jasc.com

Netscape preferences

When you have decided which text and graphics editors you prefer, write them into Netscape's Preferences panel. They can then be called up easily from within the editor.

Setting Preferences

1   In the Editor, or any other Netscape window, open the **Options** menu and select **Editor Preferences**.

2   Go to the **General** panel.

3   Click the **Browse** button by the **HTML source** slot and locate your text editor. NotePad and WordPad should both be in the *Windows* folder, and are called *Notepad.exe* and *Write.exe*.

4   Click the **Browse** button by the **Image** slot and locate your graphics editor. What, and where it is depends on your system!

5   Click **OK** to save the preferences and close the dialog box.

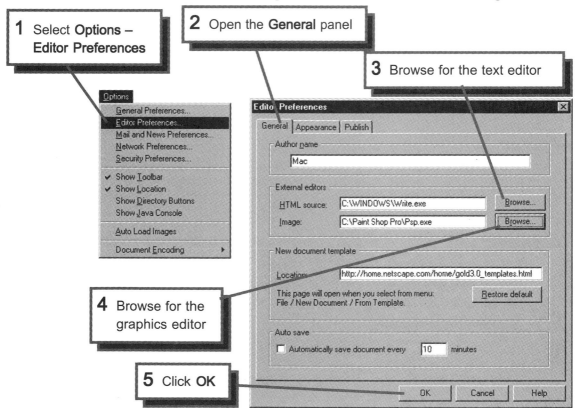

1 Select **Options – Editor Preferences**

2 Open the **General** panel

3 Browse for the text editor

4 Browse for the graphics editor

5 Click **OK**

After setting these Preferences, your chosen text editor will be called up, and the document passed to it when you select the **View – Edit Document Source** command.

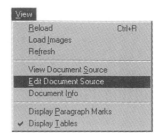

The graphics package will likewise be opened when you click the **Edit Image** button in an image's **Property** dialog box.

Network Preferences

There is one more Preference to set up before the system is ready for work with JavaScript.

1   Select **Options – Network Preferences**.

2   Open the **Languages** panel.

3   Make sure that **Enable JavaScript** is turned on!

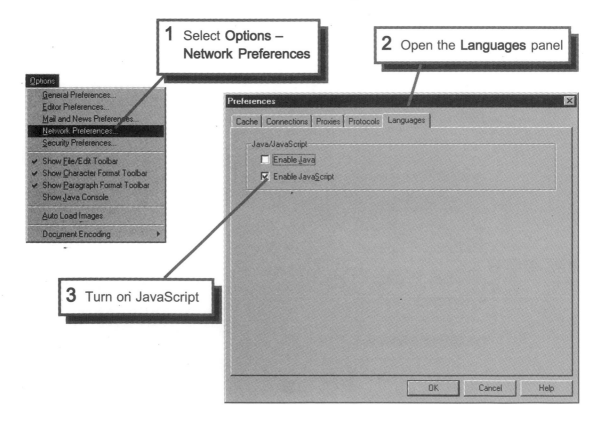

1   Select **Options – Network Preferences**

2   Open the **Languages** panel

3   Turn on JavaScript

Test your system

Before you go any further, write and run the next script to make sure that your system has everything in place and working properly.

The script is about as simple as they come. The only JavaScript here is the single instruction at the end of the <INPUT TYPE... line:

onClick = "self.status = 'Thank you for clicking'"

When you click the button, the script makes a message appears in the status bar.

The rest of the document is standard HTML code to put the button on the screen. Don't worry about how it works at this stage – all will become clear soon enough. Just type it in carefully, paying special attention to the quotes in the script. The message is enclosed in 'single quotes', and the whole of the instruction is enclosed in "double quotes". They are essential.

1   Start up your text editor – I used WordPad for this example.

2   Type in the code as shown here. The <INPUT TYPE... line can be typed in as one continuous line or split at any space – both HTML and JavaScript ignore any surplus spaces and end of line markers.

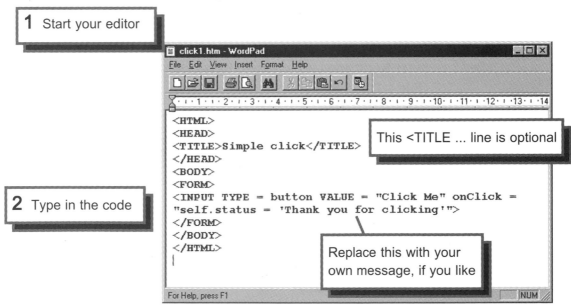

1 Start your editor

2 Type in the code

This <TITLE ... line is optional

Replace this with your own message, if you like

```
<HTML>
<HEAD>
<TITLE>Simple click</TITLE>
</HEAD>
<BODY>
<FORM>
<INPUT TYPE = button VALUE = "Click Me" onClick =
"self.status = 'Thank you for clicking'">
</FORM>
</BODY>
</HTML>
```

3   Open the **File** menu and select **Save As**. If you are using WordPad, you will be asked if you want to lose the formatting – you do! Select **Text Document**.

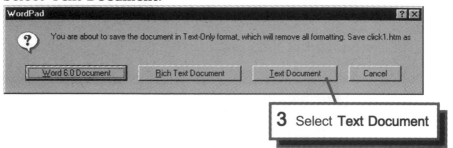

3 Select **Text Document**

4   At the **Save As** dialog box, give the file a name with the extension **.HTM** (or **.htm**), and store it in your JavaScript files folder.

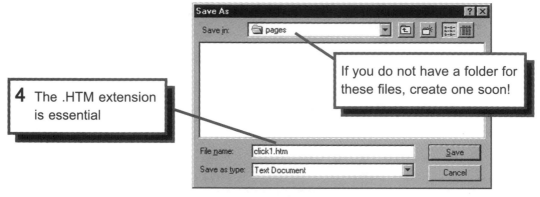

If you do not have a folder for these files, create one soon!

4 The .HTM extension is essential

5   Start **Netscape** and use the **File – Open File in Browser** command (**File – Open Page** in Navigator 4.0) to open your file.

6   Click the button!

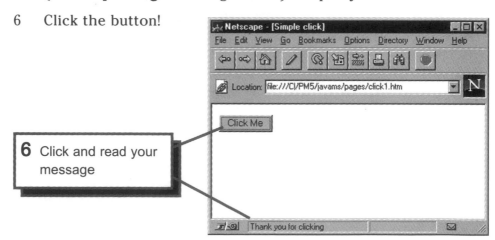

6 Click and read your message

Whoops!

If no button appears, there is a flaw in the HTML part of the code. The most likely errors here are mis-spelt tags – the words in <brackets>.

If there is an error in your JavaScript code, you will get this Alert box when you click the button. The message will vary – this was caused by typing the single and double quote in the wrong order at the end.

```
Netscape - [Alert]                                          _ □ ✕

JavaScript Error: file:/C|/PM5/javams/pages/click1.htm, line 7:

unterminated string literal.

self.status = 'Thank you for clicking
..............^

                        [ OK ]
```

Use the information in the Alert box to help you to locate the problem. Sometimes it will pinpoint the error exactly. At other times it will at least guide you in the right direction.

In this case, the error message **unterminated string literal** tells us that there is a chunk of text that is missing its end quote. Below this a portion of the code, with an arrow pointing to the start of the error. The line that this came from is identified at the top of the box.

If you do hit a problem, read the Alert box, click OK to close it, then go back to your editor, check the code carefully against the example and edit as necessary. Save the file and reload it into Netscape.

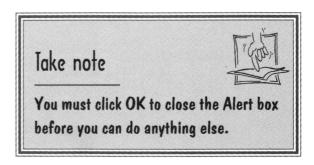

Take note

You must click OK to close the Alert box before you can do anything else.

Help from Netscape

There isn't room in this book to go into all the intricacies of the JavaScript language – and not a lot of point at this level. However, if you do want to know more details about any feature of the language there is a good guide available, on-line at Netscape.

1 Start **Netscape** and get on-line.

2 Open the **Help** menu and select **Handbook**. This will link you to the relevant page at Netscape's home site.

3 At the Handbook's opening page, select **JavaScript Guide**.

4 Use the **Contents** list, down the left, to navigate through the pages, or click the **Index** button to track down any special item.

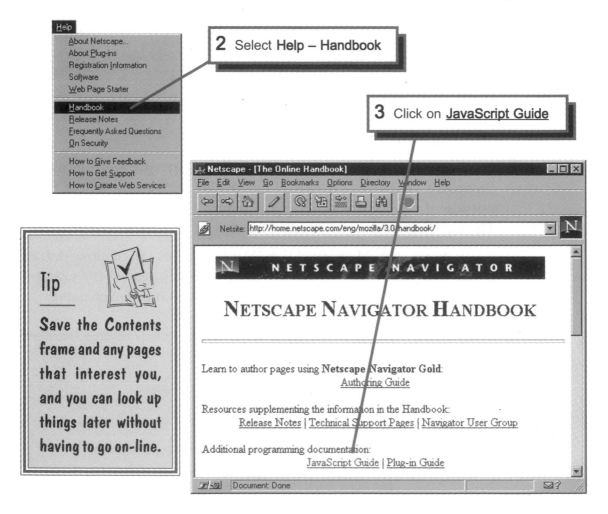

Tip

Save the Contents frame and any pages that interest you, and you can look up things later without having to go on-line.

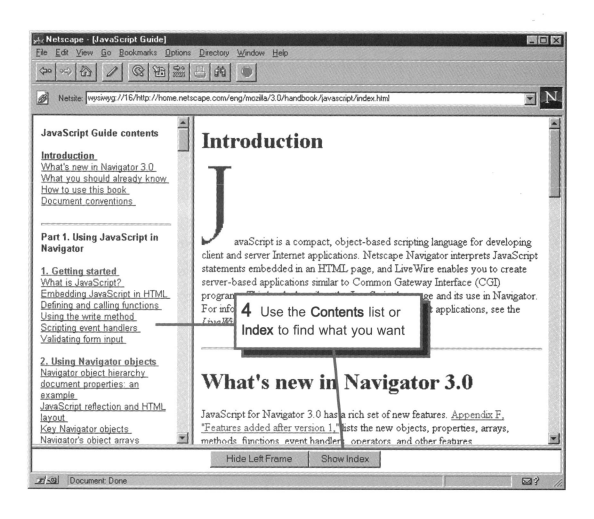

Introduction

J avaScript is a compact, object-based scripting language for developing client and server Internet applications. Netscape Navigator interprets JavaScript statements embedded in an HTML page, and LiveWire enables you to create server-based applications similar to Common Gateway Interface (CGI) programs. This includes both the JavaScript language and its use in Navigator. For info... applications, see the *LiveWi...*

> **4** Use the **Contents** list or **Index** to find what you want

What's new in Navigator 3.0

JavaScript for Navigator 3.0 has a rich set of new features. Appendix F, "Features added after version 1," lists the new objects, properties, arrays, methods, functions, event handlers, operators, and other features.

JavaScript Guide contents

Introduction
What's new in Navigator 3.0
What you should already know
How to use this book
Document conventions

Part 1. Using JavaScript in Navigator

1. Getting started
What is JavaScript?
Embedding JavaScript in HTML
Defining and calling functions
Using the write method
Scripting event handlers
Validating form input

2. Using Navigator objects
Navigator object hierarchy
document properties: an example
JavaScript reflection and HTML layout
Key Navigator objects
Navigator's object arrays

Hide Left Frame   Show Index

Take note

If you want more help, ideas, sample scripts, or discussions of JavaScript, there are plenty of links at Yahoo. Start at: http://www.yahoo.com/

Then take the menu selections

Computers and Internet –> Programming Languages –> JavaScript

Exercises

1　If you haven't got Netscape 3.0 or Communicator, go and get one now! Go for the Gold version of 3.0, or the minimum version of Communicator – you probably only need the Navigator (browser), Composer (editor) and Mail components. You can download them from:

　　http://www.netscape.com

or wherever you see the **Netscape Now!** sticker on a Web page.

Both can be downloaded free for evaluation, but you are expected to register and pay for your copy if you decide to continue to use it.

2　Create a page containing two (or more) buttons, each of which displays a different Status line message when clicked.

Save it as 'buttons.htm' and view it in Netscape.

2 Instant HTML

HTML

HTML – HyperText Markup Language – is the system used to produce Web pages. Essentially, it is a set of tags (codes) that specify text styles, draw lines, display images, handle URL links and the other features that create Web pages. It is not difficult to use. There are only a limited number of tags and they follow fairly strict rules. All tags are enclosed in <angle brackets> to mark them off from the text, and they are normally used in pairs – one at the start and one at the end of the text that they affect. For example:

```
<H1> This is a main heading </H1>
```

Notice that the closing tag is the same as the opener, except that it has a forward slash at the start.

All pages have the same outline structure:

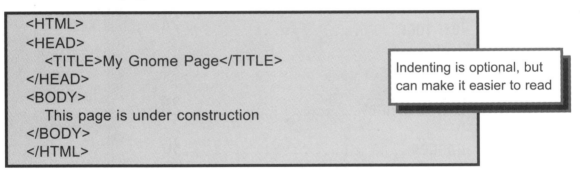

```
<HTML>
<HEAD>
   <TITLE>My Gnome Page</TITLE>
</HEAD>
<BODY>
   This page is under construction
</BODY>
</HTML>
```

Indenting is optional, but can make it easier to read

The whole text is enclosed by **<HTML>** and **</HTML>** tags.

The **<HEAD>** area holds information about the page, and is not displayed – though the Title does appear in the browser's Title bar when loaded. This can be left blank.

The **<BODY>** area is where the main code goes.

Take note

You can format text and insert images, links and tables using the Netscape editor. However, you still need to understand the tags and structure of HTML to be able to incorporate JavaScript into your pages.

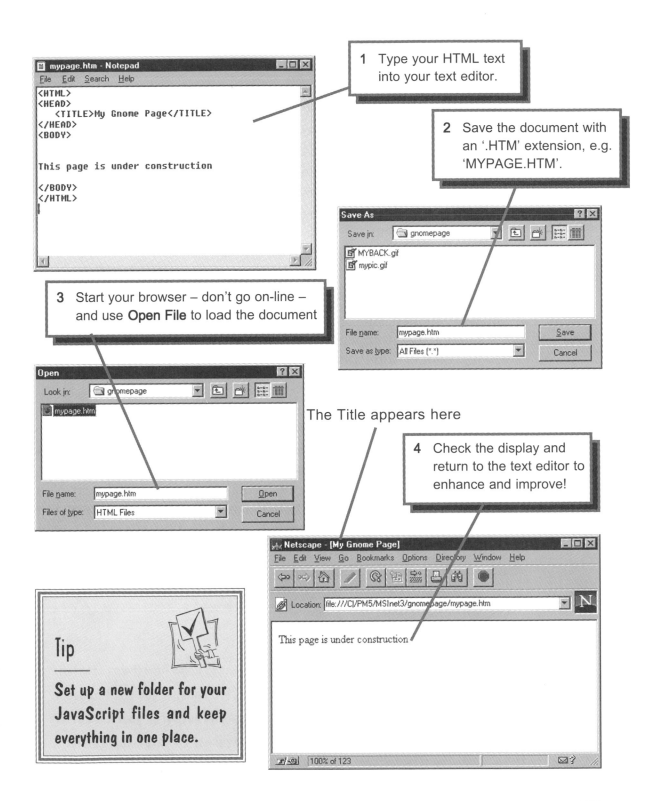

1 Type your HTML text into your text editor.

mypage.htm - Notepad

File   Edit   Search   Help

```
<HTML>
<HEAD>
   <TITLE>My Gnome Page</TITLE>
</HEAD>
<BODY>


This page is under construction

</BODY>
</HTML>
```

2 Save the document with an '.HTM' extension, e.g. 'MYPAGE.HTM'.

Save As

Save in: gnomepage

MYBACK.gif
mypic.gif

File name: mypage.htm   Save

Save as type: All Files (*.*)   Cancel

3 Start your browser – don't go on-line – and use **Open File** to load the document

Open

Look in: gnomepage

mypage.htm

File name: mypage.htm   Open

Files of type: HTML Files   Cancel

The Title appears here

4 Check the display and return to the text editor to enhance and improve!

Tip

Set up a new folder for your JavaScript files and keep everything in one place.

Netscape - [My Gnome Page]

File   Edit   View   Go   Bookmarks   Options   Directory   Window   Help

Location: file:///C|/PM5/MSInet3/gnomepage/mypage.htm

This page is under construction

100% of 123

Text tags

The simplest tags are the ones that format text. These will produce six levels of headings, a small, italicised style (mainly used for e-mail addresses), and bold and italic for emphasis.

<H1>	</H1>	Heading 1
<H2>	</H2>	Heading 2
<H3>	</H3>	Heading 3
<H4>	</H4>	Heading 4
<H5>	</H5>	Heading 5
<H6>	</H6>	Heading 6
<B>	</B>	Bold
<I>	</I>	Italic
<Address>	</Address>	Small italic style

The Heading and Address tags break the text up into separate lines, but untagged text appears as a continuous stream – no matter how you lay it out in NotePad. Create separate paragraphs with these tags:

<P>	Start a new paragaph
</P>	End of paragraph (optional)
 	Line break – use to create larger gaps

When a browser reads an HTML document, it ignores all spaces (apart from a single space between words), tabs and new lines. What this means is that it doesn't matter how you layout your HTML text. You can indent it, and add line breaks to make it easier for you to read, but it won't affect what your readers see – only the tags affect the layout of the page in the browser.

Tip

If you come across a great Web page and want to know how it was created, use View – Document Source to see the HTML code. If you want to use a page as a model for your own, use File Save As to save it on your hard disk. You can then open it and edit it. Any images must be saved separately.

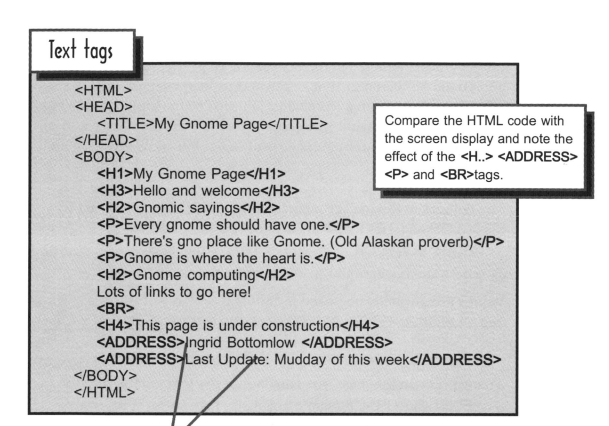

Text tags

```
<HTML>
<HEAD>
    <TITLE>My Gnome Page</TITLE>
</HEAD>
<BODY>
    <H1>My Gnome Page</H1>
    <H3>Hello and welcome</H3>
    <H2>Gnomic sayings</H2>
    <P>Every gnome should have one.</P>
    <P>There's gno place like Gnome. (Old Alaskan proverb)</P>
    <P>Gnome is where the heart is.</P>
    <H2>Gnome computing</H2>
    Lots of links to go here!
    <BR>
    <H4>This page is under construction</H4>
    <ADDRESS>Ingrid Bottomlow </ADDRESS>
    <ADDRESS>Last Update: Mudday of this week</ADDRESS>
</BODY>
</HTML>
```

Compare the HTML code with the screen display and note the effect of the **<H..>** **<ADDRESS>** **<P>** and **
** tags.

Why do each of these lines need tags at both ends? What would happen if the two were enclosed in a single set of **<ADDRESS>** **</ADDRESS>** tags?

Take note

In the code on this page and in the rest of this chapter, new tags are picked out in bold.

25

Colours

Colours are defined by the values of their Red, Green and Blue components – given in that order and in hexadecimal digits. These values can be anything from 00 to FF, with 00 meaning off, 80 is half power and FF gives full power.For example, **FFFF00** gives Red and Green at full, with no Blue. The resulting colour is Yellow.

BODY colours

The colours of the background and text of the page can be set by the **BGCOLOR** and **TEXT** options in the **BODY** tag.

    <BODY BGCOLOR = "#FFFFFF" TEXT = "#008000">

This sets the background to White and the text to Green.

Values are normally enclosed in "quotes" with a # at the start. These can be omitted **TEXT = 008000** works just as well.

FONT COLOR

At any point on the page, you can change the text colour with the tag:

    <FONT COLOR = "#Value">

The colour is used for all following text until it is reset with another **COLOR** tag. You can use it to pick out words within normal text – though you can get strange results if you use the tags inside Headings.

Colour names and RGB values

JavaScript recognises over 100 pre-defined colours. You can use these by giving their names, rather than the Red Green Blue values. e.g. **COLOR = silver** has the same effect as **COLOR = "#C0C0C0"**.

Here are some of the more useful pre-defined colours.

R	G	B	Name	R	G	B	Name
00	00	00	black	80	00	00	maroon
80	80	80	gray	FF	00	00	red
C0	C0	C0	silver	00	80	80	teal
FF	FF	FF	white	80	00	80	purple
00	00	80	navy	80	80	00	olive
00	00	FF	blue	00	FF	FF	aqua
00	80	00	green	FF	00	FF	fuchsia
00	FF	00	lime	FF	FF	00	yellow

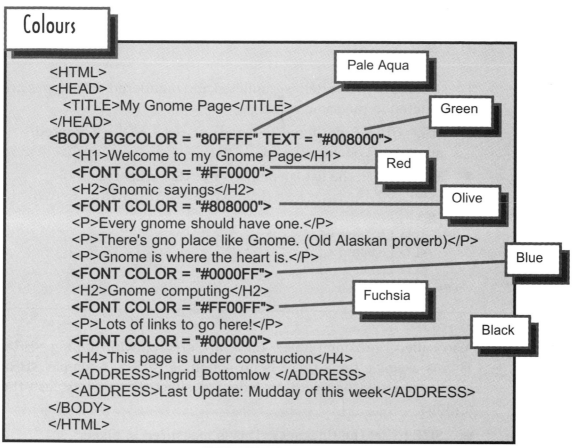

Colours

```
<HTML>
<HEAD>
  <TITLE>My Gnome Page</TITLE>
</HEAD>
<BODY BGCOLOR = "80FFFF" TEXT = "#008000">
    <H1>Welcome to my Gnome Page</H1>
    <FONT COLOR = "#FF0000">
    <H2>Gnomic sayings</H2>
    <FONT COLOR = "#808000">
    <P>Every gnome should have one.</P>
    <P>There's gno place like Gnome. (Old Alaskan proverb)</P>
    <P>Gnome is where the heart is.</P>
    <FONT COLOR = "#0000FF">
    <H2>Gnome computing</H2>
    <FONT COLOR = "#FF00FF">
    <P>Lots of links to go here!</P>
    <FONT COLOR = "#000000">
    <H4>This page is under construction</H4>
    <ADDRESS>Ingrid Bottomlow </ADDRESS>
    <ADDRESS>Last Update: Mudday of this week</ADDRESS>
</BODY>
</HTML>
```

Labels pointing to the code:
- Pale Aqua → BGCOLOR = "80FFFF"
- Green → TEXT = "#008000"
- Red → FONT COLOR = "#FF0000"
- Olive → FONT COLOR = "#808000"
- Blue → FONT COLOR = "#0000FF"
- Fuchsia → FONT COLOR = "#FF00FF"
- Black → FONT COLOR = "#000000"

Shame this book is in black and white! Still, it does help to make the point that you must have a good contrast in shade – as well as in hue – between your text and the background colour.

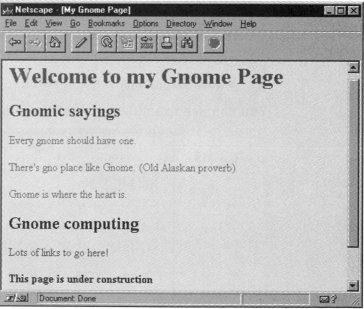

27

Lists and lines

Lists

These come in two varieties – bulleted and numbered. Both types are constructed in the same way.

● **<UL> </UL>** (unordered/bulleted) or **<OL> </OL>** (ordered/numbered) enclose the whole list.

● Each item in the list is enclosed by **<LI> </LI>** tags,

e.g.

```
<UL>
    <LI> List item </LI>
    <LI> List item </LI>
    <LI> List item </LI>
</UL>
```

Lines

Also called Horizontal Rules, these are created with the tag **<HR>**. This is a single tag – there is no matching **</HR>**. A simple **<HR>** produces a thin line with an indented effect. For variety, use the options:

● **SIZE** to set the thickness. This is measured in pixels.

● **WIDTH** can also be set in pixels, but is best given as a percentage of the width of the window – you don't know how big your readers' windows will be.

● **NOSHADE** makes the line solid.

You can see examples of all of these opposite.

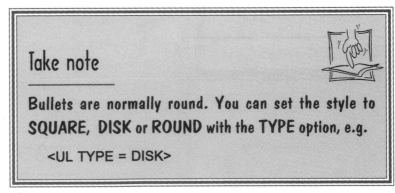

Take note

Bullets are normally round. You can set the style to SQUARE, DISK or ROUND with the TYPE option, e.g.

```
<UL TYPE = DISK>
```

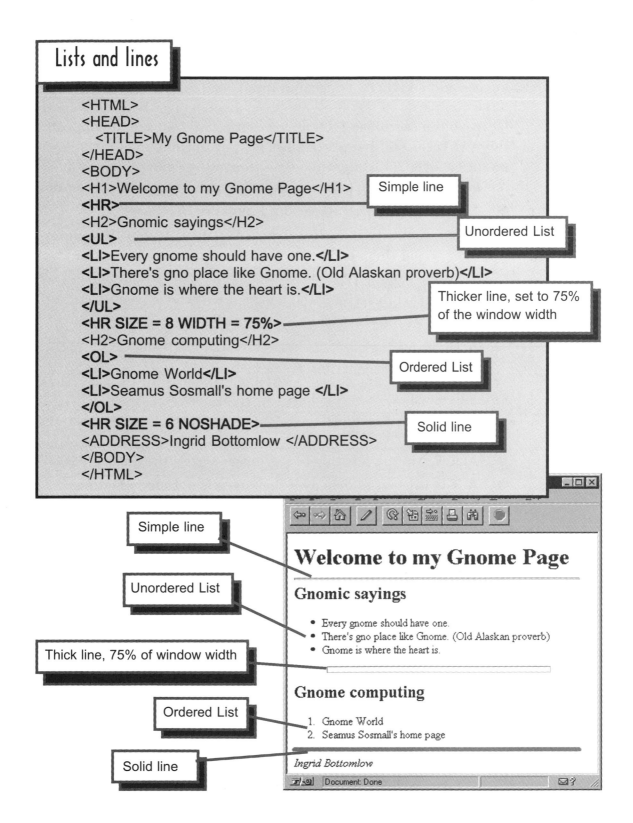

Lists and lines

```html
<HTML>
<HEAD>
   <TITLE>My Gnome Page</TITLE>
</HEAD>
<BODY>
<H1>Welcome to my Gnome Page</H1>
<HR>
<H2>Gnomic sayings</H2>
<UL>
<LI>Every gnome should have one.</LI>
<LI>There's gno place like Gnome. (Old Alaskan proverb)</LI>
<LI>Gnome is where the heart is.</LI>
</UL>
<HR SIZE = 8 WIDTH = 75%>
<H2>Gnome computing</H2>
<OL>
<LI>Gnome World</LI>
<LI>Seamus Sosmall's home page </LI>
</OL>
<HR SIZE = 6 NOSHADE>
<ADDRESS>Ingrid Bottomlow </ADDRESS>
</BODY>
</HTML>
```

Simple line

Unordered List

Thicker line, set to 75% of the window width

Ordered List

Solid line

Simple line

Unordered List

Thick line, 75% of window width

Ordered List

Solid line

Welcome to my Gnome Page

Gnomic sayings

- Every gnome should have one.
- There's gno place like Gnome. (Old Alaskan proverb)
- Gnome is where the heart is.

Gnome computing

1. Gnome World
2. Seamus Sosmall's home page

Ingrid Bottomlow

Document: Done

Images

Images add greatly to a page, but there is a cost. Image files are very large compared to text files, and even small images will significantly increase the downloading time for a page. In the example opposite, the text takes 600 bytes – almost instant downloading – while the picture is over 26Kb and will take 10 seconds or more to come in. So, include images, but keep your visitors happy by following these rules:

- Keep the images as small as possible;

- If you want to display large images – perhaps your own photo gallery, put them on separate (linked) pages and tell your visitors how big they will be.

- Include text describing the image, for the benefit of those who browse with AutoLoad Images turned off.

The basic image tag is:

    <IMG SRC = "filename">

You can also use these options:

    ALIGN = "left/center/right"
    ALT = "description"

- **ALIGN** sets the position of the image across the page.

- **ALT** is the text to display if the image is not loaded into a browser. In the example opposite, if image loading was turned off, you would see this: ⬚ A picture of me

Background images

You can tile a page with the **BACKGROUND = "filename"** option in the **<BODY>** tag. The image is repeated to fill the window.

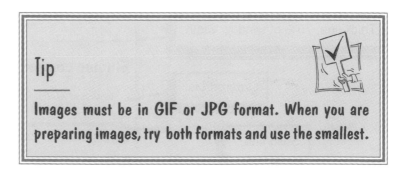

Tip

Images must be in GIF or JPG format. When you are preparing images, try both formats and use the smallest.

Images

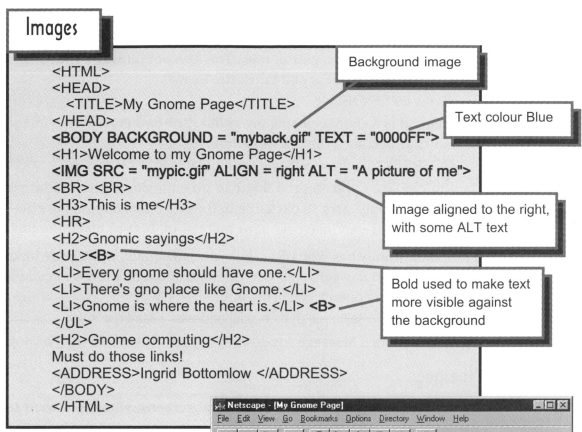

```
<HTML>
<HEAD>
  <TITLE>My Gnome Page</TITLE>
</HEAD>
<BODY BACKGROUND = "myback.gif" TEXT = "0000FF">
<H1>Welcome to my Gnome Page</H1>
<IMG SRC = "mypic.gif" ALIGN = right ALT = "A picture of me">
<BR> <BR>
<H3>This is me</H3>
<HR>
<H2>Gnomic sayings</H2>
<UL><B>
<LI>Every gnome should have one.</LI>
<LI>There's gno place like Gnome.</LI>
<LI>Gnome is where the heart is.</LI> <B>
</UL>
<H2>Gnome computing</H2>
Must do those links!
<ADDRESS>Ingrid Bottomlow </ADDRESS>
</BODY>
</HTML>
```

Background image

Text colour Blue

Image aligned to the right, with some ALT text

Bold used to make text more visible against the background

The trick with background images is to use one which doesn't clash too much with the text. Very pale or bright images and black text work well. In this example, the background image is the same as the main picture, but smaller and with fewer, paler colours – and if it was even simpler and paler, the text would be more readable.

Links

A link is created with a pair of tags. The first contains the URL of the page or file to be linked, and takes the form:

<A HREF=URL>

The second is a simple closing tag **</A>**. The two enclose the image or text that becomes the clickable link. e.g.

<A HREF= "http://www.gnomeworld.gn">Gnome World </A>

As you can see opposite, the link can be embedded within a larger item of text – only '**here**' is clickable in the *IT's Made Simple here* line. You can also use an image with, or instead of, text to make the link.

The example only has Web URLs, but you can equally well create links to FTP files and newsgroups. You can also add a link to give readers an easy way to contact you. This line:

<A HREF = "mailto:me@my.e-mail.address"> Mail me </A>

opens a **New Mail Message** window, with your address in the **To:** slot.

Links within the page

If you have a page that runs over several screens, you might want to include links within the page, so that your readers can jump from one part to another. The clickable link follows the same pattern as above, but you must first define a named place, or anchor, to jump to.

<A NAME = Top>This is the start of something big </A>

The anchor tags can fit round any text or image, and you can even leave it blank in between if you like.

The **HREF** tag is slightly different for a jump.

<A HREF = #Top> Return to top of page </A>

Notice the # before the name. This is essential.

Take note

"Quotes" are only needed round values where the value consists of more than one word. Name = "Top" and Name = Top both work.

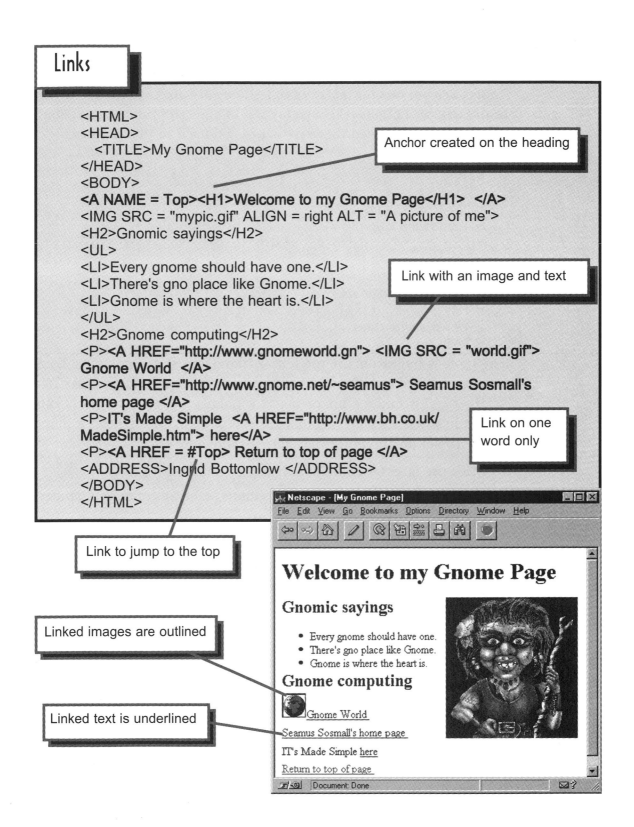

```
<HTML>
<HEAD>
   <TITLE>My Gnome Page</TITLE>
</HEAD>
<BODY>
<A NAME = Top><H1>Welcome to my Gnome Page</H1>  </A>
<IMG SRC = "mypic.gif" ALIGN = right ALT = "A picture of me">
<H2>Gnomic sayings</H2>
<UL>
<LI>Every gnome should have one.</LI>
<LI>There's gno place like Gnome.</LI>
<LI>Gnome is where the heart is.</LI>
</UL>
<H2>Gnome computing</H2>
<P><A HREF="http://www.gnomeworld.gn"> <IMG SRC = "world.gif">
Gnome World  </A>
<P><A HREF="http://www.gnome.net/~seamus"> Seamus Sosmall's
home page </A>
<P>IT's Made Simple  <A HREF="http://www.bh.co.uk/
MadeSimple.htm"> here</A>
<P><A HREF = #Top> Return to top of page </A>
<ADDRESS>Ingrid Bottomlow </ADDRESS>
</BODY>
</HTML>
```

Anchor created on the heading

Link with an image and text

Link on one word only

Link to jump to the top

Linked images are outlined

Linked text is underlined

Netscape - [My Gnome Page]

File Edit View Go Bookmarks Options Directory Window Help

Welcome to my Gnome Page

Gnomic sayings

- Every gnome should have one.
- There's gno place like Gnome.
- Gnome is where the heart is.

Gnome computing

Gnome World

Seamus Sosmall's home page

IT's Made Simple here

Return to top of page

Document: Done

Tables

Tables are not just for tables of data. They are also a convenient way to present sets of images, or to lay out images and related text. For a simple table, you need three pairs of tags, used in this pattern:

```
<TABLE>
<TR>
<TD>Row 1, Item  1</TD>
<TD> Row 1, Item  2</TD>
... across the columns
</TR>
<TR>
<TD> Row 2, Item  1</TD>
... across the columns
</TR>
... down all the rows
</TABLE>
```

The table is built from the top left, working across the columns. Each item is enclosed in <TD> </TD> tags, and each row is enclosed in <TR> </TR> tags. It takes a lot of tags to make a big table! This is one situation where I would recommend using Netscape's editor. It much easier to set up and enter data into a table with this.

1   Use the **Insert – Table** command, or click the Table icon 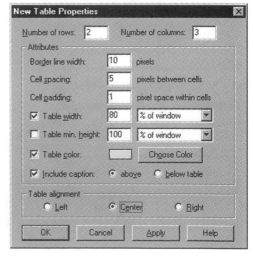.

2   Set the number of rows and columns – the size can be changed later if necessary.

3   You can set the width of borders, colours, alignment, etc. now, or leave these until later.

4   Click **OK** to close box.

5   Click into each cell in turn and type in your text or insert an image.

6   When you want to format the table, or a row or cell, right click for the menu and select **Table Properties**. Rows and columns can also be inserted or deleted from this menu.

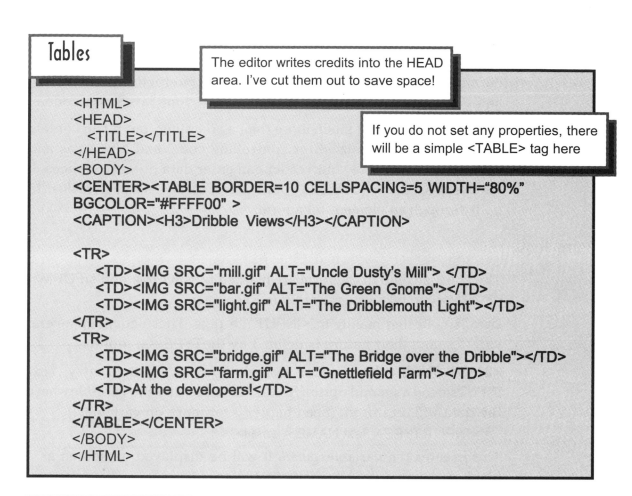

Tables

The editor writes credits into the HEAD area. I've cut them out to save space!

If you do not set any properties, there will be a simple <TABLE> tag here

```html
<HTML>
<HEAD>
   <TITLE></TITLE>
</HEAD>
<BODY>
<CENTER><TABLE BORDER=10 CELLSPACING=5 WIDTH="80%"
BGCOLOR="#FFFF00" >
<CAPTION><H3>Dribble Views</H3></CAPTION>

<TR>
   <TD><IMG SRC="mill.gif" ALT="Uncle Dusty's Mill"> </TD>
   <TD><IMG SRC="bar.gif" ALT="The Green Gnome"></TD>
   <TD><IMG SRC="light.gif" ALT="The Dribblemouth Light"></TD>
</TR>
<TR>
   <TD><IMG SRC="bridge.gif" ALT="The Bridge over the Dribble"></TD>
   <TD><IMG SRC="farm.gif" ALT="Gnettlefield Farm"></TD>
   <TD>At the developers!</TD>
</TR>
</TABLE></CENTER>
</BODY>
</HTML>
```

Take note

The Netscape Gold editor has an odd bug – it tends to shrink images when you insert them into tables. Be prepared to edit the document and remove the WIDTH and HEIGHT settings.

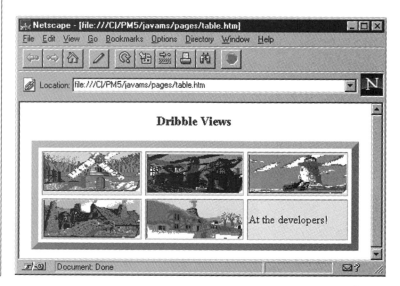

Forms

Forms are crucial to JavaScript. They are the interactive part of HTML and the link between you, your readers and your JavaScript code.

The Form itself is not much more than a container, but it can contain buttons, that can be used for controlling code, and text areas and other elements where your reader can enter data or make choices. If you want to give feedback to your reader, then it is by far easiest to do it through an element on a form.

Form tags

The start and end of the form are marked by **<FORM>** and **</FORM>**. **<FORM>** can take several options – see page 38.

Data is collected mainly in **<INPUT ...>** tags. These come in several vareties, and their nature is defined by the **TYPE =...** option.

<INPUT TYPE = text creates a single line slot for text entry. Text INPUTs need a second option **NAME =...** to identify the *variable* where the data will be stored. (See Chapter 3 for more on variables.)

    <INPUT TYPE = text NAME = email>

This creates the variable *email.* It will be displayed on screen as a blank data entry slot, 20 characters wide.

<INPUT TYPE = button creates a clickable button. The simplest way to run a JavaScript program is from one of these.

    <INPUT TYPE = button VALUE = "Done">

The **VALUE= "Done"** option defines the label for the button.

If you want to collect some text that ran over several lines, such as a snail mail address, you can use the **<TEXTAREA...>** tags.

    <TEXTAREA NAME = Address>

This displays as a very small box with scroll bars to the right and bottom. You can make it into a decent size by adding the options **ROWS** and **COLS** to define the size of the display.

    <TEXTAREA NAME = Address ROWS = 4 COLS = 40>

Simple form

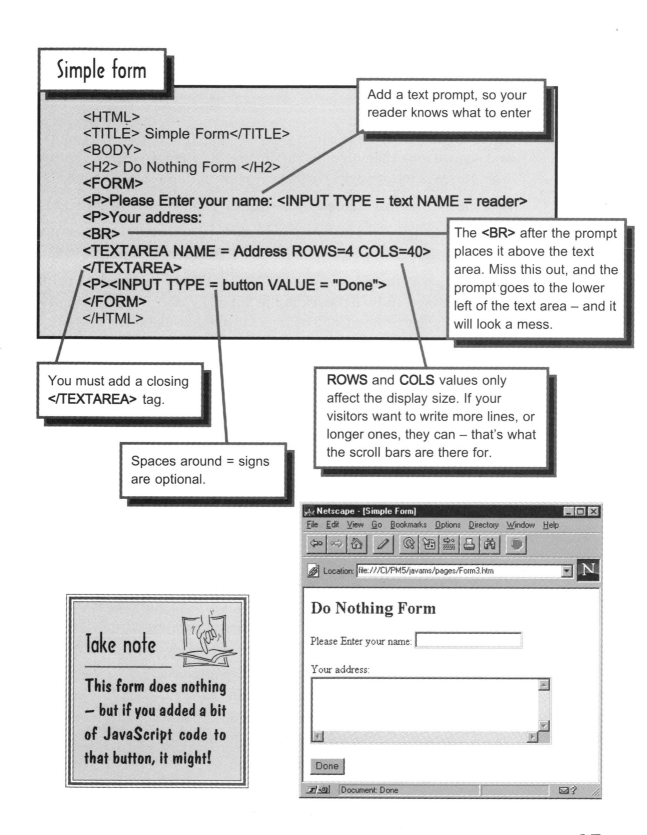

```
<HTML>
<TITLE> Simple Form</TITLE>
<BODY>
<H2> Do Nothing Form </H2>
<FORM>
<P>Please Enter your name: <INPUT TYPE = text NAME = reader>
<P>Your address:
<BR>
<TEXTAREA NAME = Address ROWS=4 COLS=40>
</TEXTAREA>
<P><INPUT TYPE = button VALUE = "Done">
</FORM>
</HTML>
```

Add a text prompt, so your reader knows what to enter

The **
** after the prompt places it above the text area. Miss this out, and the prompt goes to the lower left of the text area – and it will look a mess.

You must add a closing **</TEXTAREA>** tag.

Spaces around = signs are optional.

ROWS and **COLS** values only affect the display size. If your visitors want to write more lines, or longer ones, they can – that's what the scroll bars are there for.

Take note

This form does nothing – but if you added a bit of JavaScript code to that button, it might!

Netscape - [Simple Form]

File Edit View Go Bookmarks Options Directory Window Help

Location: file:///C)/PM5/javams/pages/Form3.htm

Do Nothing Form

Please Enter your name:

Your address:

Done

Document: Done

37

Choices

Drop-down lists

There are several ways in which you can offer choices to your readers, and we will look them in detail in Chapter 8, when we explore Forms from the JavaScript angle. One way is shown in the sample opposite.

Drop-down lists are created with **<SELECT...>** and **<OPTION =...>**.

<SELECT...> provides the framework. It needs a **NAME** to define the variable where the choice will be stored. **</SELECT>** closes the list.

Each entry is defined by an **<OPTION = ...>**. This must have a word inside the tag – to be fed back in the SELECT NAME variable – and a label to display on the list. The tags fit together like this:

```
<SELECT NAME = Level>
    <OPTION = stand> Standard
    <OPTION = prof> Professional
</SELECT>
```

That gives us a drop-down list with two items. If the visitor selects *Standard*, the *stand* option will be passed to *Level*, and the feedback mail will include this phrase:

```
Level = stand
```

Feedback by e-mail

You can set up the form so that your readers can e-mail the contents back to you after they have finished filling it in. (This only works if the reader is using Netscape, but then, the same is true of JavaScript.)

The opening **<FORM>** tag must be extended to include the keywords **METHOD** and **ACTION**, along with your e-mail address, like this:

```
<FORM METHOD = Post ACTION = mailto:your_address>
```

Somewhere in the form you need a **Submit** button.

```
<INPUT TYPE = Submit VALUE = "Send Now">
```

The option **TYPE = Submit** defines it as a button that submits feedback.

There is a similar INPUT option, Reset, which also creates a button, but this one clears the form's contents.

```
<INPUT TYPE = Reset VALUE = "Clear the Form">
```

```
<HTML>
<TITLE> Form with feedback</TITLE>
<BODY>
<H2> Contact SuperSoft </H2>
<P>For more details of our software, please complete this form

<FORM METHOD = Post ACTION = mailto:macbride@tcp.co.uk>
<P>E-mail: <INPUT TYPE = text NAME = email SIZE = 30>
<P>Real name and address:
<BR><TEXTAREA NAME = Address ROWS = 4 COLS = 40>
</TEXTAREA>
<P>Platform:
<SELECT NAME = Platform>
<OPTION = Pcdos > PC/DOS
<OPTION = Mac> Mac
<OPTION = Win> PC/Windows
</SELECT> <P>
<INPUT TYPE = Submit VALUE = "Send">
<INPUT TYPE = Reset VALUE = "Clear the Form">
</FORM>
</HTML>
```

Use **SIZE = ...** giving the number of characters to set the width

Take note

HTML is quite tolerant. Spaces around the = sign are optional. Quotes around strings in the TYPE =, NAME =, OPTION =, VALUE = expressions are only needed if the string contains more than one word.

Checkboxes and Radios

The versatile **INPUT** tag offers two more ways to let your visitors choose from alternatives. Set the **TYPE** to:

☑ **Checkbox**, if several selections can be made at once

◉ **Radio**, if only one of the set can be selected

With Checkboxes, each **INPUT** should have a **NAME** which acts as a variable to identify the selection.

```
Which types of links would you like:
<BR><INPUT TYPE = Checkbox NAME = search>Search engines
<BR><INPUT TYPE = Checkbox NAME = softsites> Software sites
<BR><INPUT TYPE = Checkbox NAME = resources> JavaScript resources
```

If the visitor selects the *Software sites* checkbox, the feedback from this form will show the variable *softsites* with the value *on*.

With Radio buttons, all the radios in the set must have the same **NAME**, but we now need to add the **VALUE** = clause. This sets the value to be returned, so that the feedback will be in the form of *mlist= yes*. If you omit the VALUE =, the feedback would read *mlist= on*, whatever was selected.

```
<P>Join our mailing list?
<BR><INPUT TYPE = Radio NAME = mlist VALUE = yes > Yes please
<BR><INPUT TYPE = Radio NAME = mlist VALUE = no CHECKED> No thanks
```

Notice the keyword **CHECKED** at the end of the second **<INPUT...** in this set. This sets the default. Miss it out if you want to start with all the Radios clear.

Take note

SELECT lists, Checkboxes and Radios are all handled slightly differently if you want to read their values from JavaScript, rather than through a feedback form. See Chapter 8.

Checkboxes and radios

```
<HTML>
<BODY>
<FORM METHOD = Post ACTION = mailto:macbride@tcp.co.uk>

Which types of links would you like:
<BR><INPUT TYPE = Checkbox NAME = search>Search engines
<BR><INPUT TYPE = Checkbox NAME = softsites> Software sites
<BR><INPUT TYPE = Checkbox NAME = resources> JavaScript resources

<P>Join our mailing list?
<BR><INPUT TYPE = Radio NAME = mlist VALUE = y > Yes please
<BR><INPUT TYPE = Radio NAME = mlist VALUE = n CHECKED> No thanks
<P><INPUT TYPE = Submit VALUE = "Send">
<P><INPUT TYPE = Reset VALUE = "Clear the Form">

</FORM>
</BODY>
</HTML>
```

Same NAME for a set of radios

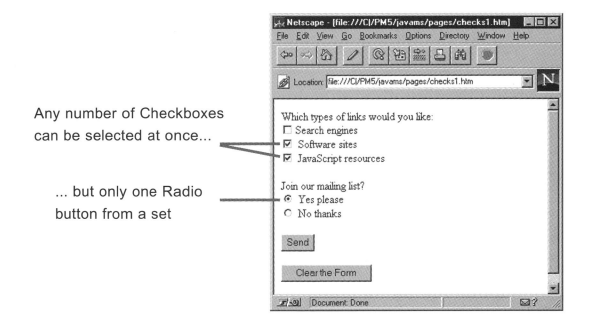

Any number of Checkboxes can be selected at once...

... but only one Radio button from a set

41

Frames

Frames add flexibility to your display and are far easier to use than you might at first think. A framed system has two types of document:

● **Layout documents** divide the screen to create the frames.

● **Content documents** go into the frames. They are identical to normal pages, though you may need to adjust their links if the pages are to call each other up within the frame window.

A layout document can divide a window vertically or horizontally – but not both. However, a frame can hold another layout document, which can subdivide vertically or horizontally. Frames can be nested within one another to any level, but the practical limit is two or three layout documents and half a dozen content frames in a screen.

The frame structure does not have to remain fixed. You can load a new layout document into a frame, or into the whole window, to give a different structure – and to link to new sets of contents documents.

<FRAMESET...>

This is used in a layout document to define the division of the window.

> **<FRAMESET ROWS / COLS = Value, Value,...>**

You can divide by **ROWS** or **COLS** – but not both. Each division needs a *Value*. These can be given in three ways:

Fixed sets the width or depth of a frame in pixels:

> ROWS = 150,...

Percent sets the width or depth as a percentage of the window size:

> COLS = 25%, ...

Relative sets the width or depth as a fraction of the remaining area. The symbol '*' used by itself simply means 'the rest of the space':

> ROWS = 200,*

This sets up two frames, the first 200 pixels deep, the second taking up whatever space is left below.

> ROWS = 100, 25%, *

This creates three horizontal frames. The top one is 100 pixels deep, the second is 25% of the height, and the third is whatever space is left.

<FRAME SRC = ... NAME = ...>

The **<FRAME...>** tag specifies the document to be displayed when the frame is first opened, and gives the frame a name. (The name is used when new documents are loaded into the frame later, and can be omitted if the contents never change.)

    <FRAME SRC = welcome.htm NAME = main>

This frame will display the *welcome.htm* file when it first opens, and may have other pages directed into it later.

The tag can also takes these options:

NORESIZE Fixes the size of the frame.

SCROLLING = Yes/No/Auto Turns scrollbars on (Yes), off (No), or leaves it to the system to switch them on when needed (Auto).

The following code will only work if you have files called *logo.htm* and *welcome.htm*. Without them, you will get messages complaining about the missing files, but the frame structure will still be visible.

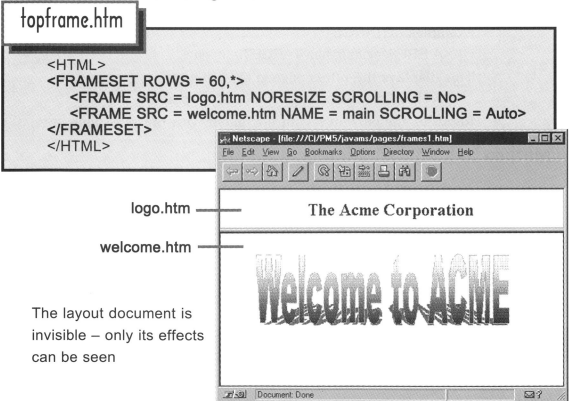

topframe.htm

```
<HTML>
<FRAMESET ROWS = 60,*>
    <FRAME SRC = logo.htm NORESIZE SCROLLING = No>
    <FRAME SRC = welcome.htm NAME = main SCROLLING = Auto>
</FRAMESET>
</HTML>
```

logo.htm ⎯⎯⎯

welcome.htm ⎯⎯⎯

The Acme Corporation

Welcome to ACME

The layout document is invisible – only its effects can be seen

43

Frames and targets

When you create a link from an ordinary page, the linked page simply replaces the calling one. When you link from a frame, the linked page can be displayed in several different places. The destination is set by the **TARGET** option in the **<A HREF ...>** tag.

    <A HREF = "url" TARGET = ...>

There are five alternative targets for the linked page:

framename displays the page in a frame identified by name in a
    <FRAME SRC = ... NAME = *framename*> tag

_self replaces the calling page in the current frame. (Omitting the
    TARGET has the same effect.)

_parent replaces the containing layout document with the new page
    – which may be a layout document, giving a new structure.

_top replaces the whole window, with the new page.

_blank opens a new Netscape window and displays the page there.
    You can have as many windows open at once as you like!

Examples of **TARGET**s:

    <A HREF = offers.htm TARGET = main>

This displays the *offers* page in the *main* frame.

    <A HREF = newframe.htm TARGET = _parent>

Replaces the current layout document with the *newframe* one.

Navigation bars and display frames

Most framed systems will use one of the frames as a 'navigation bar' – essentially a collection of links to the different pages in the set. This could be incorporated into a name and logo frame at the top of the page, or have a frame to itself.

The three-frame system illustrated opposite is easy to implement, but gives you a flexible display. At the very simplest, write your links *only* in the navigation bar, and target all pages into the main display area. If you want to add links to the contents pages, so each can call the next, omit the TARGET, so that they are loaded into the main display area.

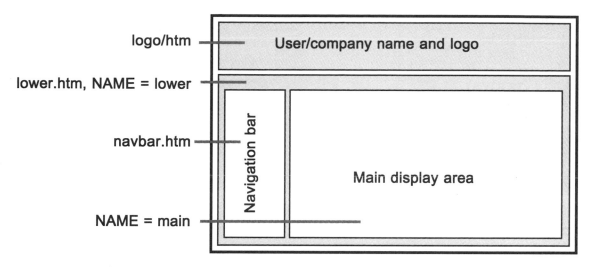

logo/htm	User/company name and logo
lower.htm, NAME = lower	
navbar.htm	Navigation bar / Main display area
NAME = main	

If you need more space for a page, use **TARGET = _parent** to fill the whole of the lower area. At the end of this page, you will need to reload the lower.htm file (and with it, the navigation bar), by a line such as:

<A HREF = lower.htm TARGET = _self> Return to the Index </A>

If you want to load a page into the full screen, with **TARGET = _top**, its return link must reload the outer layout document, to rebuild the whole of the frame system.

<A HREF = outer.htm > Return to the Home Page </A>

Three-frame example

These pages will produce a three-frame display, plus some sample 'contents' pages. These are blank apart from the links. When you save them, use the same file names or the links won't work. Start with topframe.htm, from page 41, then create these:

lower.htm

```
<HTML>
<FRAMESET COLS = 30%,*>
    <FRAME SRC = navbar.htm NORESIZE SCROLLING = Yes>
    <FRAME SRC = welcome.htm NAME = main SCROLLING = Auto>
</FRAMESET>
</HTML>
```

navbar.htm

```
<HTML>
<HEAD>
</HEAD>
<BODY>
<H2>Contents</H2>
<P><A HREF = compinfo.htm TARGET = main>About Acme</A>
<P><A HREF = sales.htm TARGET = main>Acme Products</A>
<P><A HREF = offers.htm TARGET = _parent>Special offers</A>
<P><A HREF = acmeuser.htm TARGET = _top>Acme User Group</A>
</BODY>
</HTML>
```

The first two links open their pages in the main display area; **offers.htm** goes into the lower frame and **acmeuser.htm** replaces the whole window

compinfo.htm

```
<HTML>
<HEAD>
<TITLE>About Acme</TITLE>
</HEAD>
<BODY>
This page is under construction.
<P><A HREF = sales.htm TARGET = _self>Next page</A>
</BODY>
</HTML>
```

sales.htm follows the same pattern as **compinfo.htm**

TARGET = **_self** can be omitted – either way the new page simply replaces this one in the main display area

offers.htm

```
<HTML>
<BODY>
This page is under construction.
<P><A HREF = lower.htm TARGET = _self>Return to Index</A>
</BODY>
</HTML>
```

```
<HTML>
<BODY>
This page is under construction.
<P><A HREF = outer.htm TARGET = _top>Return to main page</A>
</BODY>
</HTML>
```

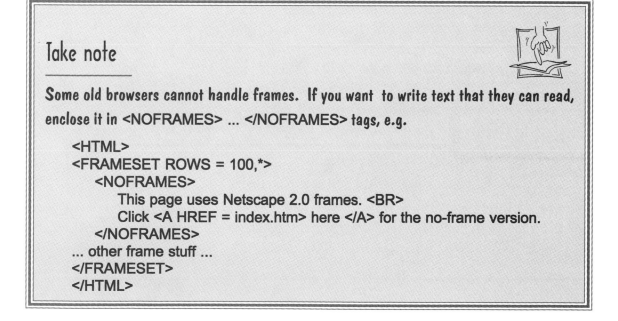

Take note

Some old browsers cannot handle frames. If you want to write text that they can read, enclose it in <NOFRAMES> ... </NOFRAMES> tags, e.g.

```
<HTML>
<FRAMESET ROWS = 100,*>
    <NOFRAMES>
        This page uses Netscape 2.0 frames. <BR>
        Click <A HREF = index.htm> here </A> for the no-frame version.
    </NOFRAMES>
... other frame stuff ...
</FRAMESET>
</HTML>
```

Exercises

1   Create a page containing a <FORM> to collect feedback from visitors. It should include INPUTs for e-mail and real names, a TEXTAREA, a SELECT list of options and buttons to send and clear the form.

2   Create a simple page with links to several of your other existing pages. The links should be organised into a bulleted list.

3   Set up a <FRAME> system, with your links page occupying a slim column on the left of the window. Adapt the links so that some open into the right frame, some replace the whole frame system in the existing window and some open into a new window.

3 Simple scripts

JavaScript and HTML

JavaScript is an extension of HTML. It can be written into your pages – and run from them – in several different ways.

<SCRIPT>

The simplest method is to enclose the code in **<SCRIPT>...</SCRIPT>** tags in the **<BODY>** part of a document.

```
<SCRIPT>
    alert("Hello")
</SCRIPT>
```

When the page is opened, the code will be executed as soon as it has been downloaded. This is fine for short and simple scripts, but if the script refers to an object further down on the page, you could have problems – if that part of the page has not been downloaded when the code tries to access it, the script will crash.

Attached code

JavaScript code can be attached directly to the event handler of an HTML object, and will be executed when the event occurs.

```
<INPUT TYPE = button VALUE = "Hi" onClick = "alert('Have a nice day')">
```

In this case, the event is a click on the button, and the code will display an **Alert** message box. (See page 52 for more on event handling.)

Functions

Scripts can be written into the **<HEAD>** area. Individual lines of code will be executed as soon as they are loaded, but the code can also be written into *functions* – self-contained blocks of code.

```
<SCRIPT>
function howdo()
{
    alert("How are you?")
}
</SCRIPT>
```

The function by itself does nothing. It will be executed when it is called from a line of JavaScript in a <SCRIPT> block, or attached to an object, somewhere in the <BODY> part of the document.

The (brackets) at the end of the **function...** line are essential, and can be used to transfer information between the function and the rest of the code. See page 100 for more on functions.

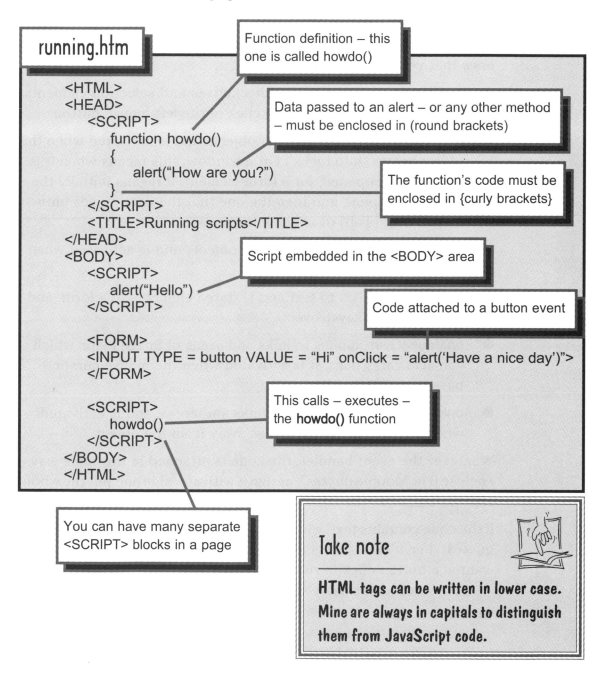

running.htm

```
<HTML>
<HEAD>
   <SCRIPT>
      function howdo()
      {
         alert("How are you?")
      }
   </SCRIPT>
   <TITLE>Running scripts</TITLE>
</HEAD>
<BODY>
   <SCRIPT>
      alert("Hello")
   </SCRIPT>

   <FORM>
   <INPUT TYPE = button VALUE = "Hi" onClick = "alert('Have a nice day')">
   </FORM>

   <SCRIPT>
      howdo()
   </SCRIPT>
</BODY>
</HTML>
```

Function definition – this one is called howdo()

Data passed to an alert – or any other method – must be enclosed in (round brackets)

The function's code must be enclosed in {curly brackets}

Script embedded in the <BODY> area

Code attached to a button event

This calls – executes – the **howdo()** function

You can have many separate <SCRIPT> blocks in a page

Take note

HTML tags can be written in lower case. Mine are always in capitals to distinguish them from JavaScript code.

Event handlers

Web pages are active and interactive, files and images load in, the user moves between frames and windows, enters text, makes selections and clicks buttons. The events can be picked up by the system and used to start JavaScript code.

There are a dozen event handlers, of which these six are probably the ones that you will use most often:

- **onClick** applies to buttons, checkboxes and selection elements on forms. It is activated by a click of the left mouse button.

- **onFocus** applies to all screen objects and is activated when the object comes 'into focus'. For a window, this means when it is opened or reopened; for a form element, it means initially the topmost element, and then the one that the user moves onto by pressing [Tab] or clicking the mouse.

- **onBlur** also applies to all screen objects and is activated when the object goes out of focus.

- **onChange** applies to text and textarea elements in a form, and picks up each keystroke.

- **onMouseOver** applies to links and areas of image maps which can also carry links. It is activated when the mouse cursor passes over the object.

- **onMouseOut** also applies to links and areas, and is activated when the mouse cursor moves away from the object.

Whatever the event handler, the code is attached in the same way – enclose it in "double quotes", assign it with an = sign and put the whole expression inside the tag that creates the object.

If the code contains text, which would normally be enclosed in double quotes, then it must be enclosed by 'single quotes' instead. So, if you wanted a button click to run the code:

```
alert("Have a nice day")
```

write it like this:

```
<INPUT TYPE = button VALUE = "Hi"
    onClick = "alert('Have a nice day')">
```

If you want to attach several JavaScript statements to an event, they should be separated by semicolons, with the whole code enclosed in double quotes as normal. This line, for example, performs the function checkEntry( ) then displays an alert message:

onClick = "checkEntry( ); alert('Thank you')"

You can respond to more than one event on an object – just leave a space, or a new line between one "*event-handler = code*" and the next. There is an example of this, and some single event code, below.

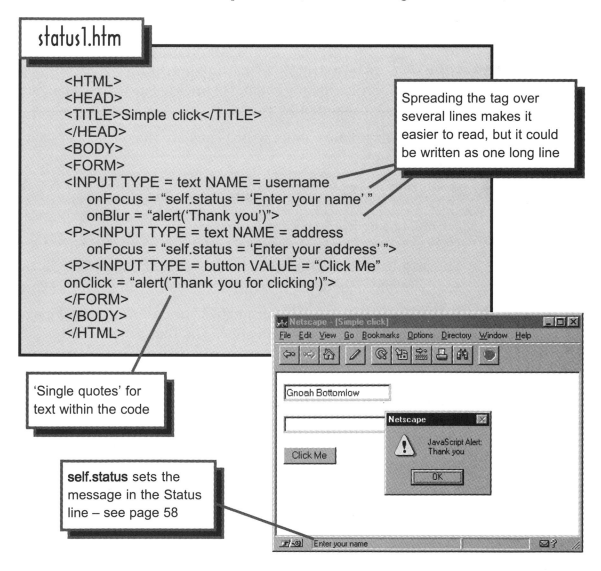

status1.htm

```
<HTML>
<HEAD>
<TITLE>Simple click</TITLE>
</HEAD>
<BODY>
<FORM>
<INPUT TYPE = text NAME = username
    onFocus = "self.status = 'Enter your name' "
    onBlur = "alert('Thank you')">
<P><INPUT TYPE = text NAME = address
    onFocus = "self.status = 'Enter your address' ">
<P><INPUT TYPE = button VALUE = "Click Me"
onClick = "alert('Thank you for clicking')">
</FORM>
</BODY>
</HTML>
```

Spreading the tag over several lines makes it easier to read, but it could be written as one long line

'Single quotes' for text within the code

self.status sets the message in the Status line – see page 58

53

write

If you want to display text on screen use the **write** method – but use it with care. **write** is similar to the print function of other languages, but has some significant differences.

The basic shape of a **write** statement is:

document.write(*expression*, *expression*, ...)

You must specify a *document*. If you are writing to the current page, then use a simple 'document'. If the output is going to a different page, you will also need to include the name of the frame or window.

DisplayFrame.document.write(...

MessageWindow.document.write(...

An *expression* can be a string of text, a number, or the value returned by a function. There can be any number of them in one write statement, but they must be separated by commas.

Note the following points about write. They are the ones most likely to give you trouble!

- **write** does not send directly to the screen, but generates HTML code, which Netscape interprets as normal before displaying. At the most basic level, this means that you have to include a <P> or <BR> tag in the write expression if you want to write on a new line. The upside of this is that you can use write to place <HR> lines, set fonts and do anything else that you can do in plain HTML.

- Where the **write** is part of a script, it will be performed as the page is loading and the output will appear on that page.

- If the **write** is attached to an object and activated by an event handler, the page display will be complete before the event can happen. When the write is performed, Netscape will open a new window and write the output there, unless it is directed to another open frame or window. In either case, the writing may well not appear until the page is reloaded!

The next example shows some of these features of **write**.

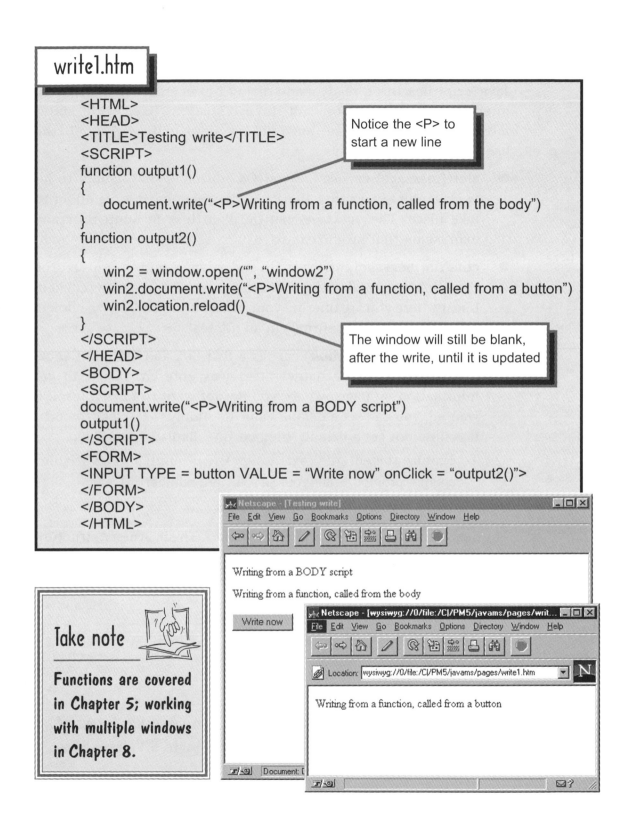

write1.htm

```
<HTML>
<HEAD>
<TITLE>Testing write</TITLE>
<SCRIPT>
function output1()
{
    document.write("<P>Writing from a function, called from the body")
}
function output2()
{
    win2 = window.open("", "window2")
    win2.document.write("<P>Writing from a function, called from a button")
    win2.location.reload()
}
</SCRIPT>
</HEAD>
<BODY>
<SCRIPT>
document.write("<P>Writing from a BODY script")
output1()
</SCRIPT>
<FORM>
<INPUT TYPE = button VALUE = "Write now" onClick = "output2()">
</FORM>
</BODY>
</HTML>
```

Notice the <P> to start a new line

The window will still be blank, after the write, until it is updated

Take note

Functions are covered in Chapter 5; working with multiple windows in Chapter 8.

Netscape - [Testing write]
File Edit View Go Bookmarks Options Directory Window Help

Writing from a BODY script

Writing from a function, called from the body

Write now

Netscape - [wysiwyg://0/file:/C|/PM5/javams/pages/writ...
File Edit View Go Bookmarks Options Directory Window Help

Location: wysiwyg://0/file:/C|/PM5/javams/pages/write1.htm

Writing from a function, called from a button

Document: [

55

Dialog boxes

JavaScript has three ready-made dialog boxes that you can use to interact with your visitors. All three display a (fixed) title and a *message*, which you can set, and hold execution of the script until the user responds.

- **alert(*message*)** carries only an **OK** button. Use it simply to let your visitors know that something has happened, or is about to take place. The *message* can be plain text in quotes, or any expression that produces text.

- **confirm(*message*)** carries an **OK** and a **Cancel** button, and returns the value **true** or **false**, depending upon which button was clicked. Use it where you are offering your visitor a simple Yes/No choice. You normally use **confirm( )** in an **if...** test.

- **prompt(*message*,*default*)** carries a text box and **OK** and **Cancel** buttons. It returns whatever text was entered. Use it to get information on pages where you do not want to have a form. If wanted, you can set a *default* value or simply "" to clear the box. If you do not set a default, the text box displays *undefined*.

  To capture the entered text, assign the prompt( ) to a variable:

  ccnum = prompt("Enter your Credit Card number","")

You can now use *ccnum* elsewhere in the code.

The next example demonstrates dialog boxes. The **if... then...** structure handles the value returned by the **confirm( )**. If **OK** is clicked, giving a **true** value, the first **alert( )** is shown; if **Cancel** is clicked, the visitor will see the "Tough..." message.

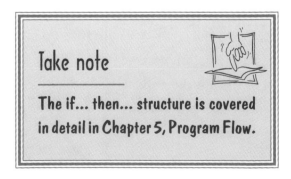

Take note

The if... then... structure is covered in detail in Chapter 5, Program Flow.

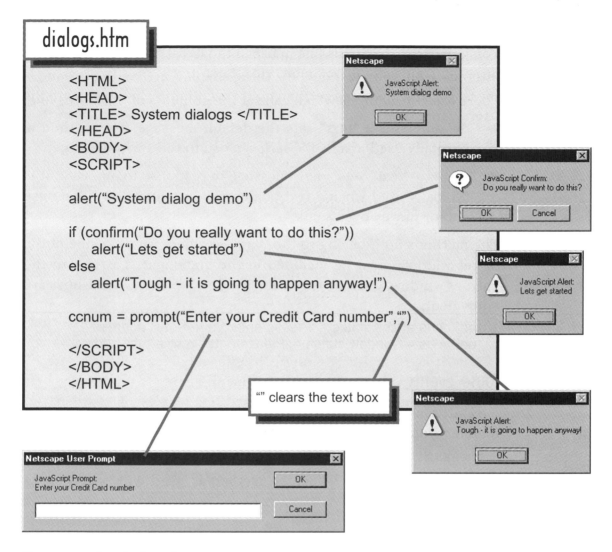

```
dialogs.htm

<HTML>
<HEAD>
<TITLE> System dialogs </TITLE>
</HEAD>
<BODY>
<SCRIPT>

alert("System dialog demo")

if (confirm("Do you really want to do this?"))
    alert("Lets get started")
else
    alert("Tough - it is going to happen anyway!")

ccnum = prompt("Enter your Credit Card number","")

</SCRIPT>
</BODY>
</HTML>
```

"" clears the text box

Home-made dialog boxes

The system dialog boxes are easy to use, but limited. You cannot change their titles, size or the fonts used within them. If you want better-looking dialog boxes, you can open a window containing your own (nicely formatted) messages and buttons. See Chapter 8 for working with windows.

The Status line

You have seen the Status line in use in the event-handler example on page 51. Time now to look more closely at it.

There are two methods which can set the contents of the Status line:

● **defaultStatus = "text"** sets the default message. The method is normally used in a BODY script, close to the start of a page.

● **status = "text"** sets a new message in response to an event. It is typically used when a text box comes into focus, or the mouse cursor moves over a link.

The methods both belong to the Window object, so the name of the target window must be included in the statement. To refer to the current window, you can use either '**window**' or '**self**'. These lines are equivalent:

```
onFocus = "self.status = 'Please enter your e-mail address' "
onFocus = "window.status = 'Please enter your e-mail address' "
```

status and mouse events

If a **status** method is run from an **onMouseOver** or **onMouseOut** event handler, you must include **"return true"** at the end of the code, e.g.

```
onMouseOver="self.status='Go to Yahoo'; return true">
```

This is not necessary when the method is used with **onFocus** or **onBlur**.

Take note

Don't rely on a simple Status line display for getting a message across to your visitor — it is very easily overlooked. A scrolling Status line is a bit more eye-catching. There's a routine for this on page 113, though the technique has been so over-used, that you may prefer to look for a different way to attract your visitors' attention.

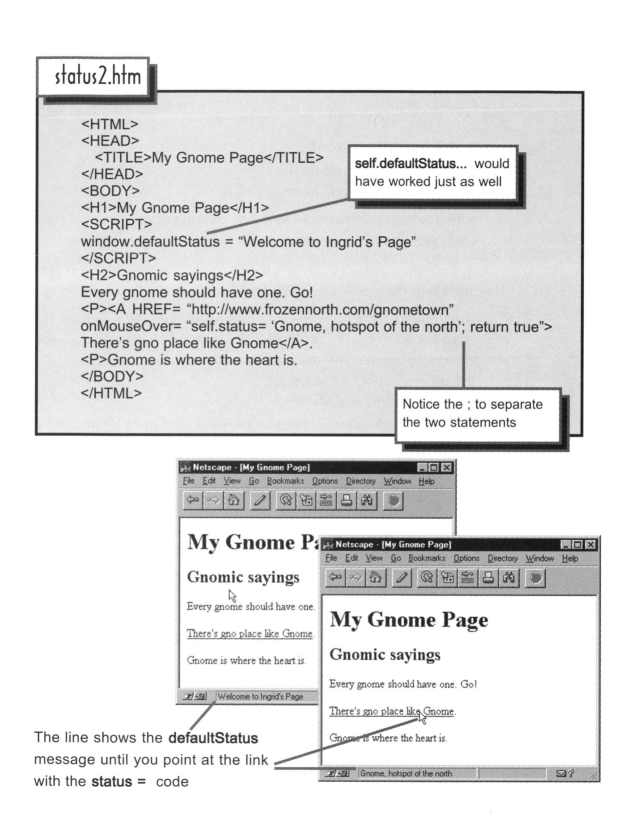

status2.htm

```
<HTML>
<HEAD>
  <TITLE>My Gnome Page</TITLE>
</HEAD>
<BODY>
<H1>My Gnome Page</H1>
<SCRIPT>
window.defaultStatus = "Welcome to Ingrid's Page"
</SCRIPT>
<H2>Gnomic sayings</H2>
Every gnome should have one. Go!
<P><A HREF= "http://www.frozennorth.com/gnometown"
onMouseOver= "self.status= 'Gnome, hotspot of the north'; return true">
There's gno place like Gnome</A>.
<P>Gnome is where the heart is.
</BODY>
</HTML>
```

self.defaultStatus... would have worked just as well

Notice the ; to separate the two statements

The line shows the **defaultStatus** message until you point at the link with the **status =** code

59

Colours

The colours of the background, normal text and links can be set from JavaScript, just as they can from HTML. The keywords are:

bgColor   background

fgColor   foreground (text)

linkColor   an unvisited link

alinkColor   link at the moment of clicking on it

vlinkColor   a visited link

Colours are properties of the document object, so you must include 'document' in the name when referring to them.

Changing colours is a neat way to emphasise the active part of the screen in a multi-frame or multi-window system. In these cases, you would have to include the name of the window and/or frame, e.g.

```
win2.document.bgColor = 'beige'
mainFrame.document.bgColor = 'silver'
```

The next example has little practical purpose, but does demonstrate colour changing. The most useful part of it is in the BODY tag, where there are colour changes attached to the **onFocus** and **onBlur** events.These dim the background to grey when the window goes out of focus, and restore the ivory background when it becomes active.

Notice the code on the last two buttons.

```
<INPUT TYPE = button VALUE = "Black"
    onClick = "document.bgColor='black'; document.fgColor = 'white'">
```

There is no point in trying to set the foreground colour from an event handler! Though the background colour can be changed at any point, the text is only written when the page is first opened, or reloaded.

```
<INPUT TYPE = button VALUE = "Reload"
    onClick = "window.location.reload()">
```

When you reload the page, it uses the default colours for the browser, or those set in the BODY tag, not the latest settings from some code.

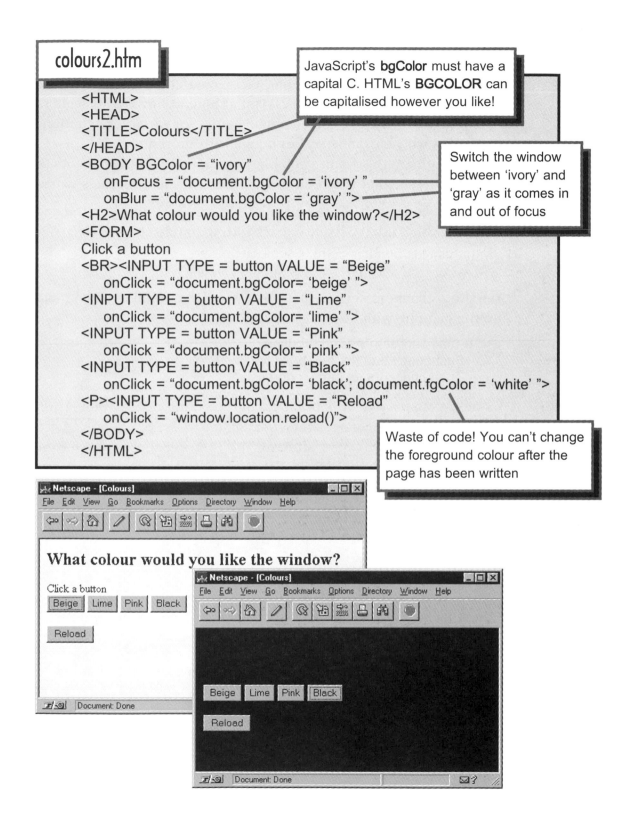

colours2.htm

```
<HTML>
<HEAD>
<TITLE>Colours</TITLE>
</HEAD>
<BODY BGColor = "ivory"
    onFocus = "document.bgColor = 'ivory' "
    onBlur = "document.bgColor = 'gray' ">
<H2>What colour would you like the window?</H2>
<FORM>
Click a button
<BR><INPUT TYPE = button VALUE = "Beige"
    onClick = "document.bgColor= 'beige' ">
<INPUT TYPE = button VALUE = "Lime"
    onClick = "document.bgColor= 'lime' ">
<INPUT TYPE = button VALUE = "Pink"
    onClick = "document.bgColor= 'pink' ">
<INPUT TYPE = button VALUE = "Black"
    onClick = "document.bgColor= 'black'; document.fgColor = 'white' ">
<P><INPUT TYPE = button VALUE = "Reload"
    onClick = "window.location.reload()">
</BODY>
</HTML>
```

JavaScript's **bgColor** must have a capital C. HTML's **BGCOLOR** can be capitalised however you like!

Switch the window between 'ivory' and 'gray' as it comes in and out of focus

Waste of code! You can't change the foreground colour after the page has been written

Netscape - [Colours]
File Edit View Go Bookmarks Options Directory Window Help

What colour would you like the window?

Click a button
Beige Lime Pink Black

Reload

Document: Done

Netscape - [Colours]
File Edit View Go Bookmarks Options Directory Window Help

Beige Lime Pink Black

Reload

Document: Done

61

Comments

Program code should be readable. When you come back to a page after a few days, weeks or months, you shouldn't have to struggle to make sense of it. The use of meaningful names for variables, functions and objects will help, and may be enough with short and simple pieces of code. With anything more complex, you should add comments to remind yourself what is stored in variables and how routines work.

There are two ways to write comments. For a short note – at the end of a line or on a line by itself – start with a double slash //

```
// num holds 5 at this point
num1++;                          // num now holds 6
```

To write a comment several lines long, start the first line with /* and end the last line with */

```
/* e-mail address checking routine
    First check that the text box contains text!
    Then check for @ in the address
    Last check for spaces and invalid characters */
```

As everything between /* and */ is ignored by Netscape, you can pretty up your comments as much as you like!

```
/* ************************************************
 * This routine calculates pi to 5,000 places      *
 * devised by Charley Farley and Piggy Malone *
 * City College, Sept - Dec 1997                   *
 *************************************************/
```

Take note

You won't find many comments in the examples in this book as I've taken them out of the code and placed them in little boxes to make them more visible. But look out for them when you view the source code of interesting pages that you find on the Web.

Coping with old browsers

Any modern browser will either be able to run JavaScript code, or will know to ignore everything between the <SCRIPT> tags. Some older browsers can't cope with JavaScript at all, and it is considered good form to write your pages with their users in mind.

To stop old browsers from displaying the code on screen, enclose it in HTML multi-line comment tags. With these, the starting '<!' must be followed by at least 2 dashes '<!--'.

    `<!-- Start a multi-line HTML comment`

The closing bracket goes on a new line after the JavaScript code. This line must start with // to make it into a JavaScript comment, and end with another 2 (or more) dashes before the end bracket '-->'.

    `// close the HTML comment with -->`

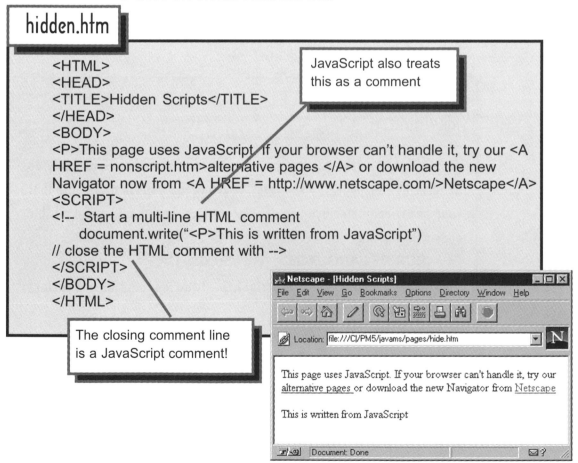

hidden.htm

```
<HTML>
<HEAD>
<TITLE>Hidden Scripts</TITLE>
</HEAD>
<BODY>
<P>This page uses JavaScript. If your browser can't handle it, try our <A
HREF = nonscript.htm>alternative pages </A> or download the new
Navigator now from <A HREF = http://www.netscape.com/>Netscape</A>
<SCRIPT>
<!-- Start a multi-line HTML comment
    document.write("<P>This is written from JavaScript")
// close the HTML comment with -->
</SCRIPT>
</BODY>
</HTML>
```

JavaScript also treats this as a comment

The closing comment line is a JavaScript comment!

Netscape - [Hidden Scripts]

File Edit View Go Bookmarks Options Directory Window Help

Location: file:///C|/PM5/javams/pages/hide.htm

This page uses JavaScript. If your browser can't handle it, try our alternative pages or download the new Navigator from Netscape

This is written from JavaScript

Document: Done

Exercises

1 The text that you output with write is processed as HTML text before display. Use this fact to produce a Web page containing at least some varied text and a horizontal line, using only **write** lines in a <SCRIPT>, and with no code in the <BODY> of the document.

2 Create a page that initially has text and background in the same colour, so that the text is hidden. Include in it a button. When this is clicked it should display a prompt, asking for a password, before changing the background to a contrasting colour.

Don't worry at this stage about checking the password.

3 Go back over your earlier page files and add comments to any parts that you feel need explaining if you are to understand them later!

Take note

JavaScript 1.1 — the version that is covered in this book — can only be handled by Netscape 3.0 and later. If you really want to make sure that your pages can be enjoyed by all your visitors, you should make all this code with the tag:

    <SCRIPT LANGUAGE = "JavaScript1.1">

then write more code — in JavaScript 1.0 — to do the same job and enclose that in the tag:

    <SCRIPT LANGUAGE = "JavaScript">

Netscape 2.0 will ignore the JavaScript 1.1 code and run the other; later versions of Netscape will ignore the 1.0 code.

Alternatively, you could just encourage visitors to upgrade their browsers!

4 Variables and values

Variables and types of data

Variables are named places in memory where you can store the data needed in your programs. You can have as many variables as you need, and call them what you like – within limits (see next page). When you compile your program, the system will allocate space for the variables, and convert the names into memory address (that the computer uses).

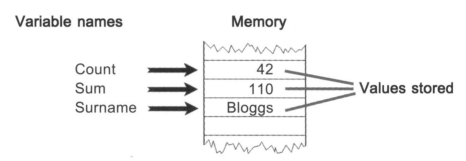

Unlike most programming languages, JavaScript does not mind what type of data you store in a variable – the same variable can be used, at different points in the code, to store numbers, text or other values. There are essentially four types of data:

- **numbers** JavaScript does not distinguish between integers (whole numbers) and those with decimal fractions – you can mix and match them as much as you like. Numbers are normally handled in the standard denary (base 10) format, though JavaScript can read values in octal, hexadecimal and other bases.

- **strings** Any text written in quotes in your code, or typed in by a user is a string. It can consist of any number of characters from 1 upwards – I haven't bothered to find out the maximum, but it is more than you will ever need.

- **Boolean values** These are either **true** or **false** – and note that the words are written without quotes. They are mainly used for carrying the results of a test from one part of the code to another.

- **null** This is a special case, and used to refer to empty strings, missing objects and other null values.

Creating variables

A variables can be set up, or *declared*, at any point in a program by the simple matter of assigning (see next page) a value to it:

```
x = 99
message = "Thank you for calling"
```

These lines set up a variable called *x* with an initial value of *99*, and one called *message* containing the string "*Thank you for calling*".

Variables can also be declared using the keyword **var**.

```
var username
var max = 500
```

The first line creates the variable *username*, but without giving it a value; the second creates *max*, and assigns *500* to it.

It is good practice to declare your variables at the start of the program or of the block of code in which they are used. When you come back to your code after a few weeks, it will be easier to understand if you can see at a glance what variables are in use and what their initial values are.

Variable names

The rules for variable names are the same as those for object names. Names must start with a letter or underscore (_) and may contain any combination of letters and digits. Spaces cannot be used, and symbols (apart from _ and $) should be avoided.

You can use either upper or lower case letters in a name, but mix them with care as JavaScript is case-sensitive. *myName*, *myname*, *MyName*, and *MYNAME* are four different things. The convention is to use capitals only at the start of following words in a multi-word name.

Keeping names reasonably short and simple will cut down typing errors, but perhaps the most important rule is to make sure that the names mean something to you!

```
ageLimit = 18
sex = "M"
var    VATdue
```

Assigning values

To assign a value to a variable, you always use the pattern:

    variable = value

The value can be a literal – some text, a number or true, false or null; another variable; a calculation or other expression; or a function that produces a value.

The scope of variables

When we talk about the **scope** of a variable we mean those parts of the code which can access the variable to use or change its value. A variable's scope depends upon how and where it was created.

- Variables declared by assignment in the <BODY> of a document have **global** scope. They can be accessed by any JavaScript anywhere else in the document – in another <SCRIPT> block, in some event code, or in a <HEAD> function. They can even be accessed from other documents by prefacing the variable's name with the document's name. *username* in *mainWindow* can be used from another window by the use of *mainWindow.username*.

- Variables declared by assignment in a function are **local** to that function. They cannot be accessed from any other code.

- Variables declared with a **var** in a function are also local to the function. Use this format if there is another variable of the same name elsewhere in the document. It ensures that the one in the function is a separate, local, variable, and that the global one will still have the same value after the function has been executed.

The following program demonstrates variable scope.

Two variables, x and y, are declared and assigned values at the start of the BODY script. The values are displayed.

The function is then called. In the function, y is declared with a **var** and values are assigned to both. The values are again displayed.

On return to the BODY script, the values are displayed one last time. x now holds the value assigned to it in the function, but y still holds its original value. The y variable in the function was a separate, local, entity. Whatever is done to that y has no effect on the other y.

vars.htm

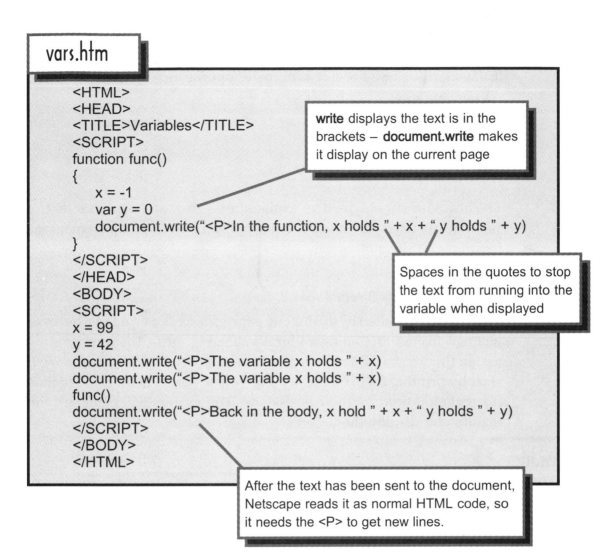

```
<HTML>
<HEAD>
<TITLE>Variables</TITLE>
<SCRIPT>
function func()
{
    x = -1
    var y = 0
    document.write("<P>In the function, x holds " + x + " y holds " + y)
}
</SCRIPT>
</HEAD>
<BODY>
<SCRIPT>
x = 99
y = 42
document.write("<P>The variable x holds " + x)
document.write("<P>The variable x holds " + x)
func()
document.write("<P>Back in the body, x hold " + x + " y holds " + y)
</SCRIPT>
</BODY>
</HTML>
```

write displays the text is in the brackets – **document.write** makes it display on the current page

Spaces in the quotes to stop the text from running into the variable when displayed

After the text has been sent to the document, Netscape reads it as normal HTML code, so it needs the <P> to get new lines.

Take note

Functions are covered in the next chapter.

Calculations

In JavaScript there are five arithmetic operators:

+   addition
–   subtraction
*   multiplication
/   division
%   modulus

The first four should need no explanation – they are used exactly the same as in ordinary arithmetic. The % operator gives you the remainder from integer division, e.g.

14 % 4 = 2

14 divided by 4 is 3 remainder 2.

The values produced by arithmetic expressions can be used wherever you can use a variable or a literal value, e.g. print them on screen, assign them to variables, or use them within other calculations. We'll start by printing them on the screen. This program displays the sums (as text) followed by the expressions. The system will calculate the results and display them.

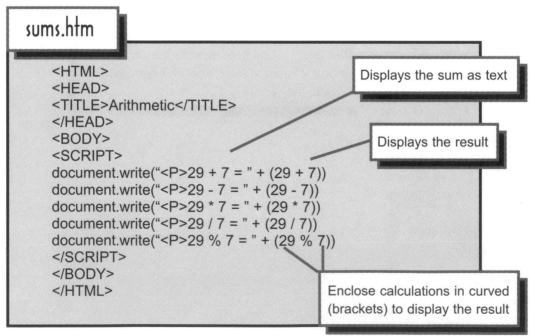

sums.htm

```
<HTML>
<HEAD>
<TITLE>Arithmetic</TITLE>
</HEAD>
<BODY>
<SCRIPT>
document.write("<P>29 + 7 = " + (29 + 7))
document.write("<P>29 - 7 = " + (29 - 7))
document.write("<P>29 * 7 = " + (29 * 7))
document.write("<P>29 / 7 = " + (29 / 7))
document.write("<P>29 % 7 = " + (29 % 7))
</SCRIPT>
</BODY>
</HTML>
```

Displays the sum as text

Displays the result

Enclose calculations in curved (brackets) to display the result

When compiled and executed, you should see this output:

```
29 + 7 = 36
29 - 7 = 22
29 * 7 = 203
29 / 7 = 4.142857142857143
29 % 7 = 1
```

Text and numbers

Notice the brackets around the calculations in the **write** expressions. They are absolutely essential. If you miss them out, so the first line, for example reads:

```
document.write("<P>29 + 7 = " + 29 + 7)
```

then this is what you get when you view the page in Netscape.

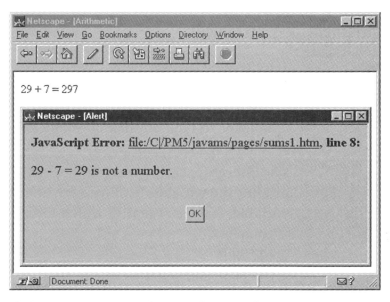

What happened? The + operator is also used to combine strings of text – or mixed text and numbers. So, in the first line, **"20 + 7 = " + 29 + 7** becomes **"20 + 7 = 297"**. In the second line, the system has already decided that **29** is to be added to the text, and is therefore treated as text, so when it hits the **- 7** it throws out the error message *29 is not a number*!

eval()

If you want to ensure that an expression is converted into a number, process it through the **eval()** method. This can be used on calculations, but is most valuable for extracting numbers from text boxes.

```
num = eval(document.form1.num1.value)
```

Assignment operators

These combine an arithmetic operator with assignment, producing a shortcut for changing the value of a variable. They look like this:

```
+=  −=  *=  /=      %=
```

and are used like this:

```
num += 2;
```

which is the same as:

```
num = num + 2;
```

You will really appreciate these with long variable names!

Increment and decrement

The ++ (increment) and −− (decrement) operators can be used to increase or decrease the value of a variable by 1.

```
num++;
```

is quicker to type but has the same effect as:

```
num = num + 1;
```

The operators can be used either prefix or postfix – i.e. written before or after the variable. If all you are doing is changing the value of that variable, it doesn't matter which form you use. These are identical:

```
num++;
++num;
```

If you are assigning the value to another variable at the same time, the position of the operator is crucial.

```
num2 = num1++;
```

assigns the inital value of **num1** to **num2**, then increments **num1**.

```
num2 = ++num1;
```

increments **num1** before assigning its value to **num2**.

You can see this at work in the next example.

```
<HTML>
<HEAD>
<TITLE>Incrementing</TITLE>
</HEAD>
<BODY>
<SCRIPT>
num1 = 5;
num1++;                        // num now holds 6
document.write("<P>num1 now = " + num1)

num2 = num1++;
// num holds 7 after assignment
document.write("<P>num1 assigned then incremented. num2 = " + num2)

num2 = ++num1;
// num holds 8 before assignment
document.write("<P>num1 incremented then assigned. num2 = " + num2)
document.write("<P>num1 now = " + num1)
</SCRIPT>
</BODY>
</HTML>
```

> Comments can be written at the end of a line, or on a separate line

This program outputs:

```
num1 now = 6
num1 assigned then incremented. num2 = 6
num1 incremented then assigned. num2 = 8
num1 now = 8
```

Tip

The longer the program and the bigger the gap between the places where a variable is used, the more likely you are to spell it wrong. Keep names simple, keep them meaningful, and be consistent in your use of capitals.

73

Operator precedence

The calculations so far have been simple ones, with only one operator. You can have Java expressions with several operators and values – just as you can on paper. The rules of precedence apply here, much as in ordinary arithmetic.

Where an expression has several operators, multiplication and division are done first, then addition and subtraction, and finally the assignment operators (though these are normally used only in simple calculations). If part of the expression is enclosed in brackets, that part is evaluated before the rest, e.g.:

2 + 3 * 4 − (9 - 3) / 2

has its bracketed operation dealt with:

2 + 3 * 4 − 6 / 2

then its multiplication and division:

2 + 12 - 3

and finally the addition and subtraction:

11

Where you have a sequence of multiplication and division (or addition and subtraction), it does not matter which you do first, e.g.:

4 * 6 / 3   =   24 / 3   =   8
or   =   4 * 2   =   8

Take note

JavaScript also has *bitwise* operators that can change the values of individual bits within a byte. They are mainly used for manipulating memory and input/output streams, and are beyond the scope of a Made Simple book.

Arrays

Arrays let you store and manipulate information in bulk. Use them wherever you have a lot of related data – list of names or URLs, sets of co-ordinates and the like.

The basic principles behind arrays are simple. Instead of having 10, 100 or 1 million or more variables each with a unique name, you have one name which refers to the whole set, with each individual *element* identified by its *subscript* – its position in the set. The subscript is written in [square brackets] after the array name.

As the subscript can be a variable, you have a simple way of accessing any – or all – the elements in the array. We will look at this properly in the next chapter when we get on to ways of repeating actions, but here's a simple example to show what is possible. Suppose you had an array of 1,000 numbers (**num**) and a variable (**count**). If you ran **count** through the full range of subscripts, while repeating this single line:

    document.write(num[count]);

it would display all the numbers in the array. If those numbers had been stored in individual variables, you would have needed 1,000 **write**s to display them! You can see this in the example overleaf – with only 8 elements, the effect is less dramatic, but the convenience of arrays is clearly demonstrated.

Initialising arrays

An array is not actually a type of variable, as it is in other languages, but an *object*. To create an array, you would use a line like this:

    product= new Array(10);

This sets up an array, called **product**. The **new** constructor (the method that creates objects) allocates memory space for 10 elements. Numbering always starts from 0, so the subscripts for the elements in this array will run from **product[0]** to **product[9]**. Notice the square [brackets] around the subscripts.

Values are assigned to array elements, just as they are to variables:

    product[0] = "Widget, small"
    product[1] = "Widget, medium"

Array methods

The Array object has several pre-defined methods which you can use on your new arrays.

- **join( )** combines all the elements of the array into one string

- **reverse( )** turns the array on its head, so that it starts with its last element and finishes with its first

- **sort( )** sorts the array into order. This is normally ascending alphabetical order though you can set it to sort descending, or numerically up or down.

To use one of these methods, simply tack its name to the name of the array – and don't forget the brackets at the end. So, to sort the products array, you would use:

```
products.sort( )
```

This next example creates an array of 8 elements and stores into it the names of the languages covered in the Made Simple series. It then outputs them in their original order, and again as a sorted list. You might like to replace my data with something of your own!

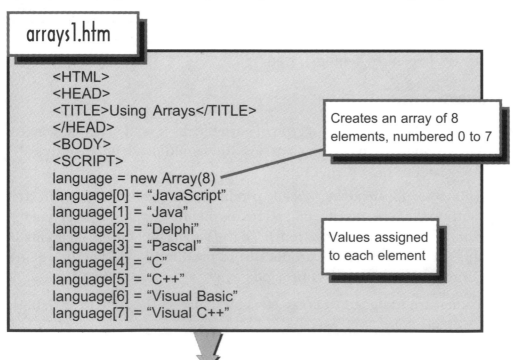

arrays1.htm

```
<HTML>
<HEAD>
<TITLE>Using Arrays</TITLE>
</HEAD>
<BODY>
<SCRIPT>
language = new Array(8)
language[0] = "JavaScript"
language[1] = "Java"
language[2] = "Delphi"
language[3] = "Pascal"
language[4] = "C"
language[5] = "C++"
language[6] = "Visual Basic"
language[7] = "Visual C++"
```

Creates an array of 8 elements, numbered 0 to 7

Values assigned to each element

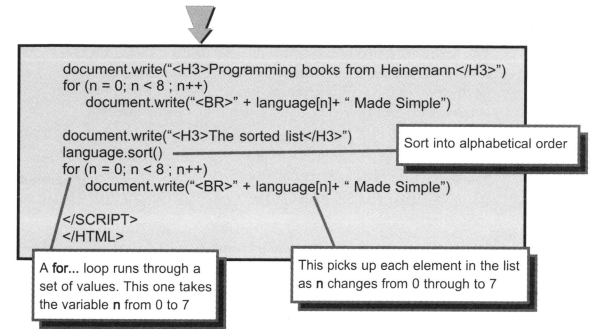

```
document.write("<H3>Programming books from Heinemann</H3>")
for (n = 0; n < 8 ; n++)
    document.write("<BR>" + language[n]+ " Made Simple")

document.write("<H3>The sorted list</H3>")
language.sort()
for (n = 0; n < 8 ; n++)
    document.write("<BR>" + language[n]+ " Made Simple")

</SCRIPT>
</HTML>
```

Sort into alphabetical order

A **for...** loop runs through a set of values. This one takes the variable **n** from 0 to 7

This picks up each element in the list as **n** changes from 0 through to 7

Tip

See the next Chapter to find out how for... loops work.

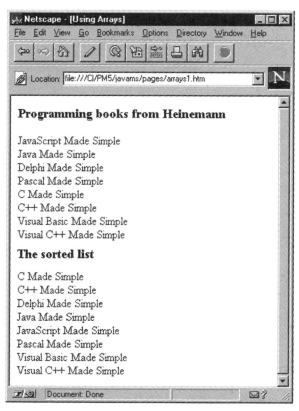

See what happens to the sort if you use a mixture of capitals and lower case letters to start the items in the array.

Arrays of elements

The text boxes, text areas, select options, buttons and other elements that you place on a form are automatically formed into an array. When each element is a totally separate item, to be treated individually, this is irrelevant, but there are times when it can be useful. If you do need to access or change the values in a set of items, treating them as array elements can be the simplest way to do it.

The array is always called *elements[]*. The elements are numbered in the order that they appear on the form – and the first one will be *elements[0]*.

In the next example, an array-based routine is used to clear the entries in a set of text boxes on the form. This allows visitors to erase the choices they have made, without also clearing their name and e-mail address. Compare this with the Reset button, which wipes all the text boxes clean.

Notice that the loop values run from 2 to 4, picking up the 'Order...' text boxes only. After you have got this working, edit the end value of the loop to read 'loop < 7' and see what happens when you let it run on to the buttons.

Take note

The images on a page are also formed into an array. See page 123 for ideas on using the images[] array.

Clear orders just wipes elements[2 to 4] – the Order text boxes

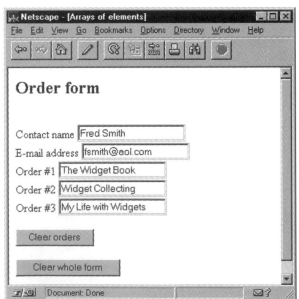

78

arrays2.htm

```
<HTML>
<HEAD>
<TITLE>Arrays of elements</TITLE>
<SCRIPT>
function clearform()
{
    for (loop = 2 ; loop < 5; loop ++)
        document.form1.elements[loop].value = ""
}
</SCRIPT>
</HEAD>
<BODY>
<H2>Order form</H2>
<FORM NAME = form1>
<BR>Contact name
<INPUT TYPE = text NAME = username VALUE = "">
<BR>E-mail address
<INPUT TYPE = text NAME = email VALUE = "">
<BR>Order #1
<INPUT TYPE = text NAME = order1 VALUE = "">
<BR>Order #2
<INPUT TYPE = text NAME = order2 VALUE = "">
<BR>Order #3
<INPUT TYPE = text NAME = order3 VALUE = "">
<P><INPUT TYPE = button VALUE = "Clear orders"
        onClick = "clearform()">
<P><INPUT TYPE = reset VALUE = "Clear whole form">
</FORM>
</BODY>
</HTML>
```

See the next chapter for more on **for...** loops

Clears the value in the looped text boxes

Standard reset button clears all text boxes, areas and selections

Tip

The elements that you are accessing should be in a continuous set so that you can run their subscripts through a loop. If you have to give subscripts individually, you might just as well access the elements by name.

79

Strings

In JavaScript, strings are not actually variables, but objects. Much of the time this does not make an awful lot of difference – you can treat them just as you would treat as variables. However, the String object has some useful properties and methods, and you can apply these to any strings in your code.

To do the job properly, a string should be created with a line such as:

```
myString = new String("This is a string")
```

In practice, a simple assignment normally works just as well:

```
myString = "This is a string"
```

Any text entered at a prompt, Text box or TextArea is also a string.

The most important *property* of a string is **length**. This tells you the number of characters. Access this with expressions of the type:

```
howlong = myString.length
```

If *myString* hold "This is a string", *howlong* would have the value 16.

There are many String methods. Most of these are used for adding HTML formatting to strings before they are written to the page, and we'll ignore those at this level. More immediately useful are these four which allow you to manipulate the string.

- **charAt(*place*)** returns the character at *place*. As with arrays, the elements (characters) of a string are numbered from 0. Run through a loop, you can use it to check each character in the string. e.g. you could look for "X" like this:

```
for(loop = 0; loop < myString.length; loop++
    if (myString.charAt(loop) == "X") ...
```

- **split(*separator*)** chops the string into pieces, splitting it where it finds a *separator* character. The pieces are passed into an array.

```
myArray = myString.split(" ")
```

This produces an array of 4 elements, "This", "is", "a", "string".

- **substring(*first,last*)** returns the set of characters, from *first* to *last*, as a new string.

```
newString = myString.substring(2,6)
```

newString now holds "is is".

- **toLowerCase( )** converts all the characters to lower case:

    document.write(myString.toLowerCase( ))

    Notice that **toLowerCase( )** has empty brackets at the end. These show that it is a method, not a property, and are essential.

- **toUpperCase( )** converts all the characters to uppercase.

Here they all are in action.

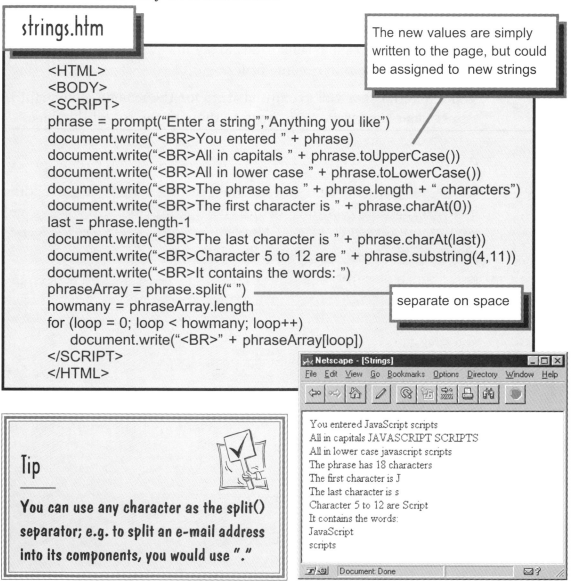

strings.htm

The new values are simply written to the page, but could be assigned to new strings

```
<HTML>
<BODY>
<SCRIPT>
phrase = prompt("Enter a string","Anything you like")
document.write("<BR>You entered " + phrase)
document.write("<BR>All in capitals " + phrase.toUpperCase())
document.write("<BR>All in lower case " + phrase.toLowerCase())
document.write("<BR>The phrase has " + phrase.length + " characters")
document.write("<BR>The first character is " + phrase.charAt(0))
last = phrase.length-1
document.write("<BR>The last character is " + phrase.charAt(last))
document.write("<BR>Character 5 to 12 are " + phrase.substring(4,11))
document.write("<BR>It contains the words: ")
phraseArray = phrase.split(" ")
howmany = phraseArray.length
for (loop = 0; loop < howmany; loop++)
    document.write("<BR>" + phraseArray[loop])
</SCRIPT>
</HTML>
```

separate on space

Netscape - [Strings]

File Edit View Go Bookmarks Options Directory Window Help

You entered JavaScript scripts
All in capitals JAVASCRIPT SCRIPTS
All in lower case javascript scripts
The phrase has 18 characters
The first character is J
The last character is s
Character 5 to 12 are Script
It contains the words:
JavaScript
scripts

Document: Done

Tip

You can use any character as the split() separator; e.g. to split an e-mail address into its components, you would use "."

81

Exercises

1   Create a page that will take in one number at a time and add it to a total. The inputs and outputs can be through dialog boxes or through <INPUT TYPE = text...> tags. You will find it simplest to attach the calculation to the **onClick( )** event of a button.

2   Using the previous document as a basis, produce a 'calculator' that will allow the user to enter two numbers, then click one of a set of buttons to add, subtract, multiply or divide those numbers.

3   Starting with the Arrays example on page 76, produce a program that will output the original (unsorted) array in reverse, then output the sorted array, again in reverse order.

4   Write a script that will prompt visitors for their name, convert it to upper case, then write a big hello to them at the top of the page.

5 Program flow

Testing values

Program flow refers to the order in which a program's instructions are carried out. So far, most of the example programs have run straight through a sequence, then stopped. There is a limit to what you can achieve with such simple programs. The addition of loops and branches makes programs far more useful and powerful.

● In a loop, a set of instructions will be repeated a fixed number of times, or until a condition is met.

● Branches take the flow off down different routes, depending upon the values held by variables.

But before we go any further, let's see how we can test values.

Relational operators

These are used to compare variables with values or with the contents of other variables. There are six relational operators:

```
== equal to        <  less than      <= less than or equal to
!= not equal to    >  greater than   >= greater than or equal to
```

Notice that the equality test uses a double equals sign '=='. The single sign '=' is used for assigning values. Typical test expressions are:

```
(x < 99)
(newNum != oldNum)
```

Tests are enclosed in brackets, and return a boolean value – **true** or **false**. You don't normally need to worry about this – just use the test – but occasionally it is useful to store the result of the test in a variable, for reference later in the program, e.g.

```
result = (newNum > oldNum)       // store the test result
...
if (result == true)              // same as if (newNum > oldNum)
```

Logical operators

The relational operators test variables against one value at a time, but you often want to check if a variable falls into a range of values, or is one of several possibilities. This is where the *logical operators* come into play.

AND and OR

The **&&** (AND) operator compares the results from two tests, with the expression being true if both tests are true.

((x >= 20) && (x <= 30))

This expression is true for all values of **x** from 20 to 30.

With an | | (OR) operator, the expression is true if either or both of the tests are true.

((x > 100) || (y > 200))

This expression is true if **x** is greater than 100 or **y** is greater than 200, or if both are over their limits.

A logical expression can have more than two tests and can include both **&&** and | |. In mixed expressions, **&&** is evaluated first, unless you use brackets – here, as in arithmetic, anything in brackets is evaluated first.

((x >= 20) && (x <= 30) || (y > 200))

For this to be true, the **x** value must be between 20 and 30, or the **y** value over 200 – in which case, the **x** value is irrelevant.

(((x > 100) || (y > 200)) && (edgecheck = true))

This is true if either, or both, the **x** and **y** values are over the limit, and **edgecheck** has been set to true.

Take note

The aim of this chapter is to explain the words that can be used to structure JavaScript programs. So that we can focus on those, and not get bogged down in other matters, the examples are all either trivial or contrived. The interesting stuff comes later, once we have got the basics out of the way!

for loops

The **for** loop allows you to repeat a set of instructions for a given number of times. The basic shape of the loop is:

```
for (var = start_value; end_test; change)
    { statement(s); }
```

When the program hits this line for the first time, *var* is assigned its *start_value*. The *statement*, or block of statements, are executed, and the flow loops back to the **for** line. The value of *var* is then adjusted as specified by the *change*. The *end_test* is performed – typically comparing *var* with a value, e.g. **counter < 100**. If *end_test* is not met, the statements are performed again, and the flow continues to loop back until it is met.

This simple **for** line:

```
for (counter = 0; counter <10 ; counter++)
```

sets up a loop that will repeat its statements a total of 10 times, as *counter* is incremented through the values 0 to 9.

The change does not have to be an increment. This loop will repeat 20 times, as counter is taken through the values 100, 95, 90, down to 0.

```
for (counter = 100; counter >0 ; counter = counter - 5)
```

The loop in this next example produces a simple times table display. Try it, then try it with different start values, end tests and changes.

forloop1.htm

```
<HTML>
<HEAD>
<TITLE>For loops</TITLE>
</HEAD>
<BODY>
<SCRIPT>
table = 7
for (n = 1; n <= 10 ; n++)
    document.write("<BR>" + (n * table))
</SCRIPT>
</HTML>
```

Blocks of code

If you want to loop through a set of instructions, not just one, enclose the statements in curly {brackets}. For example, we can extend the code to display the loop counter as well as the multiple. (This could, of course, have been done directly in the write method. Working through the *outstring* variable makes it a little easier to read.)

```
...
for (n = 1; n <= 10 ; n++)
{
    outstring = "<BR>" + n + " times " + table + " = " + (n * table))
    document.write(outstring)
}
...
```

The display is now:

```
1 times 7 = 7
2 times 7 = 14
...
```

Varying loop values

The number of times that a for loop is iterated (repeated) is determined by the start and end values, but these do not have to be fixed at design time. If either or both values are held in variables, they can be assigned by the program's user or calculated during its run.

In the next example, the end value is a random number – see the Detour, on the next page, for an explanation of that line.

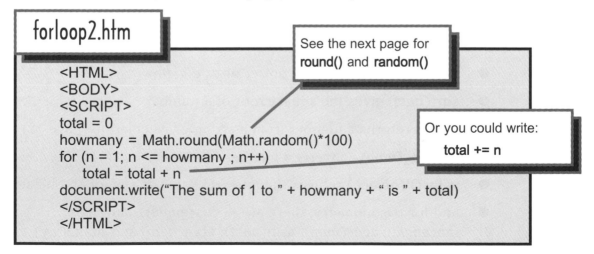

forloop2.htm

See the next page for **round()** and **random()**

Or you could write:
    total += n

```
<HTML>
<BODY>
<SCRIPT>
total = 0
howmany = Math.round(Math.random()*100)
for (n = 1; n <= howmany ; n++)
    total = total + n
document.write("The sum of 1 to " + howmany + " is " + total)
</SCRIPT>
</HTML>
```

Detour – the Math methods

JavaScript has a **Math** object which doesn't actually do anything except act as a holder for a set of methods that give extra mathematical facilities to the language. We used two of these in the last example.

Math.round() converts a number with a decimal fraction up or down to the nearest integer.

Math.random() generates a random number in the range 0.0 to 1.0. Used at its simplest, e.g.

```
x = Math.random()
```

this will give you a value between 0.0 and 1.0. If you want a decent sized number, this must be mutiplied up. Multiply by 10 and the number will be in the range of 0 to 10 – but it will still have a fractional part. If you want an integer, you must convert the expression by passing it through the **round()** method.

```
randNum = round(Math.random() * 1000))
```

randNum will be a whole number between 0 and 1000.

The other Math methods are:

- **ceil(*num*)** rounds *up* and **floor(*num*)** rounds *down* a number with a decimal fraction to the nearest integer;

- **abs(*num*)** strips off any minus sign, so abs(-4) = abs(4) = 4

- **max(*num1,num2*)** and **min(*num1,num2*)** compare two numbers and return the highest, or lowest.

- **log(*num*)** gives the logarithm of a number and **exp(*log*)** converts a logarithm back into a number.

- **pow(*n,p*)** raises *n* to the power of *p* ; e.g. pow(2,3) = 2^3 = 8

- **sqrt(*num*)** gives the square root of a number

- **eval()** returns a number from a string or calculation (page 72)

- **toString(*num*)** converts a number to a string

- **valueOf(*object*)** returns the numeric value, if any, of an object

- and for trigonometry, there are – **cos(*angle*)**, **sin(*angle*)**, **tan(*angle*)**, **acos(*num*)**, **asin(*num*)**, **atan(*num*)** and **atan2(x,y)**

Nested loops

Loops can be 'nested' inside one another, with the inner loop running its full course each time the program flow passes through the outer loop. It's a technique that you might use to read an array, or to create a table of two (or more) dimensions.

The next example creates a times table for the numbers 1 to 6, multiplying each in turn by 1 to 10. When you think that each of the loops could have a far higher end value, you realise just how much work you can get out of two or three lines of code, thanks to loops!

nesting1.htm

```
<HTML>
<HEAD>
<TITLE>Nesting1</TITLE>
</HEAD>
<BODY>
<SCRIPT>
for (table = 1; table <= 6 ; table++)
{
    for (n = 1; n <= 10 ; n++)
        document.write((n * table) + " ... ")
    document.write("<BR>")
}
</SCRIPT>
</HTML>
```

The output from this script leaves much to be desired! The problem is that the output from write is HTML code, and HTML does not support tabs or allow more than one space between items. Using dots for spacing us a crude solution. There must be a better way to create a table – as we will see on the next page.

```
Netscape - [Nesting1]
File  Edit  View  Go  Bookmarks  Options  Directory  Window  Help

1 ... 2 ... 3 ... 4 ... 5 ... 6 ... 7 ... 8 ... 9 ... 10 ...
2 ... 4 ... 6 ... 8 ... 10 ... 12 ... 14 ... 16 ... 18 ... 20 ...
3 ... 6 ... 9 ... 12 ... 15 ... 18 ... 21 ... 24 ... 27 ... 30 ...
4 ... 8 ... 12 ... 16 ... 20 ... 24 ... 28 ... 32 ... 36 ... 40 ...
5 ... 10 ... 15 ... 20 ... 25 ... 30 ... 35 ... 40 ... 45 ... 50 ...
6 ... 12 ... 18 ... 24 ... 30 ... 36 ... 42 ... 48 ... 54 ... 60 ...

Document: Done
```

Tables from loops

It is worth remembering that you can **write** any HTML tags. If you look back at the <TABLE> tags (page 34), you will see that the row, <TR>, and column data <TD> tags fall naturally into an inner and outer loop pattern. By dropping those into appropriate places in the looped lines, and adding a couple of write lines to put the start and end <TABLE> tags in place, we can create a neat HTML table.

nesting2.htm

```
<HTML>
<HEAD>
<TITLE>For loops</TITLE>
</HEAD>
<BODY>
<SCRIPT>
document.write("<TABLE BORDER=10 CELLSPACING=5 >")
for (table = 1; table <= 6 ; table++)
{
    document.write("<TR>")
    for (n = 1; n <= 10 ; n++)
        document.write("<TD>" + (n * table) + "</TD>")
    document.write("</TR>")
}
document.write("</TABLE>")
</SCRIPT>
</HTML>
```

Start the TABLE, setting options as required

Begin a new row

Add a column item

End the row

Take note

There's an alternative solution to this layout problem on page 98.

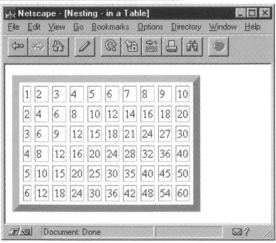

90

while loops

for loops are normally repeated for a set number of times. **while** loops give you greater flexibility in two ways:

● the exit test can check any variable, not just a loop counter;

● the exit test can be at the start or end of the loop – so, if the right condition is met, the loop's statement may not be performed at all.

The **while** loop takes this shape:

```
while (test)
{ statement(s); }
```

The system performs the test on entry to the loop, and before each repetition. Here's a very simple example, using a counter to determine the number of repetitions.

whileEx.htm

```
<HTML>
<HEAD>
<TITLE>While loop</TITLE>
</HEAD>
<BODY>
<SCRIPT>
count = 0
while (count < 10)
{
    count++
    document.write("<BR>Count = " + count)
}
</SCRIPT>
</HTML>
```

One of the things to notice here is that this displays 1 to 10, even though the text is **count < 10**. That's because the increment and print is done *after* the test. Compare this with the equivalent for loop, and keep the difference in mind when setting up loop tests.

```
for (count = 0;count < 10; count++)
        System.out.println(count);        //displays 0 to 9
```

91

break

break provides a way of escaping from **for** or **while** loops. It is essential if there is a possibility that the exit condition will *never* be met, and useful where you just need an alternative exit.

In the break demo, below, the loop allows users three chances to work out the answer to a sum. If they give the correct answer, the break forces an early exit from the loop. By checking the loop variable, count, after the end of the loop, the program can tell whether the user failed (count == 3) or got it right (early exit).

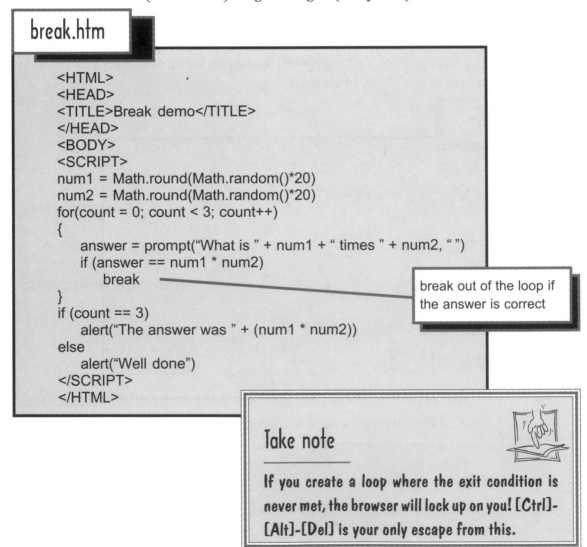

break.htm

```
<HTML>
<HEAD>
<TITLE>Break demo</TITLE>
</HEAD>
<BODY>
<SCRIPT>
num1 = Math.round(Math.random()*20)
num2 = Math.round(Math.random()*20)
for(count = 0; count < 3; count++)
{
    answer = prompt("What is " + num1 + " times " + num2, "")
    if (answer == num1 * num2)
        break
}
if (count == 3)
    alert("The answer was " + (num1 * num2))
else
    alert("Well done")
</SCRIPT>
</HTML>
```

break out of the loop if the answer is correct

Take note

If you create a loop where the exit condition is never met, the browser will lock up on you! [Ctrl]-[Alt]-[Del] is your only escape from this.

continue

continue is used in similar situations to **break**, but where **break** takes the flow right out of the loop, **continue** just skips over any remaining lines and loops round again. Use it where the lines in the lower part of the loop should only be performed if a condition is met.

continue.htm

```
<HTML>
<HEAD>
<TITLE>Continue demo</TITLE>
</HEAD>
<BODY>
<SCRIPT>
num1 = 99
while (num1 != 0)
{
    num1 = prompt("Enter first number or 0 to exit"," ")
    if (num1 == 0)
        break
    num2 = prompt("Enter second number", " ")
    if (num2 == 0)
    {
        alert("0 entered. Restart sum")
        continue
    }
    ans = num1 * num2
    alert("Multiplied = " + (num1 * num2))
}
</SCRIPT>
</HTML>
```

No point in mutiplying by 0. Go back and get another pair of numbers

An **if ...** structure (next page) will have the same effect on the flow:

```
if (num != 0)
    {
        ans = num1 * num2
        alert("Multiplied = " + (num1 * num2))
    }
```

but **continue** is neater where there are a lot of lines to jump over.

Branching with if

Loops make programs powerful, giving them the ability to process masses of data. Branches make them flexible, allowing them to vary their actions in response to incoming data. The simplest form of branch uses the **if** structure. This is the basic syntax:

```
if (test)
    { statement(s) if true}
```

The test checks the value held by a variable. **if** the test proves true, the program performs the statement(s), otherwise they are ignored.

A variation on this uses the **else** keyword, which handles the actions to perform if the test does not proves true. The syntax is:

```
if (test)
    { statement(s) if true}
else
    { statement(s) if false}
```

For example:

```
if (age < 18)
    { cost = 3.50}
else
    { cost = 5.00}
```

Under 18's get in for £3.50. Everybody else pays £5.00.

You can see the **if** structure at work in the next example. It gets the computer to work out the value of a random number, which it does by splitting the difference between the highest and lowest possible values. If its 'guess' is too high, or too low, a message is displayed and the upper or lower limits adjusted.

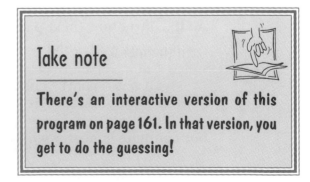

Take note

There's an interactive version of this program on page 161. In that version, you get to do the guessing!

```
<<HTML>
<HEAD>
<TITLE>Guess</TITLE>
</HEAD>
<BODY>
<SCRIPT>
x = Math.round(Math.random()*100)
max = 100
min = 0
count = 0
guess = Math.round((max + min) / 2)
while (guess != x)
{
    document.write("<BR>Trying " + guess)
    count++
    if (guess > x)
    {
        document.write(" Too high")
        max = guess
    }
    if (guess < x)
    {
        document.write(" Too low")
        min = guess
    }
    guess = Math.round((max + min) / 2)
}
document.write("<BR>It was " + guess + " Found it in " + count + " goes.")
</SCRIPT>
</HTML>
```

Results in a number half way between the upper and lower limits

We must assign a value to guess before starting the while loop, then again before it loops back

Here's a typical output – the computer never takes more than seven goes. Why not?

Netscape - [Guess]

File Edit View Go Bookmarks Options Directory Window Help

Trying 50 Too low
Trying 75 Too low
Trying 88 Too high
Trying 82 Too high
It was 79 Found it in 4 goes.

Document: Done

Multiple branching

The basic **if** structure has the beauty of simplicity – it shows clearly the relationship between the test and the outcome. However, it is not always the best solution. Consider this problem. You want to analyse a characters to see if it is an upper or lower case letter, digit or a symbol. Here's the first draft of a program to do the job.

chars1.htm

```
<HTML>
<HEAD>
<TITLE>Character testing1</TITLE>
</HEAD>
<BODY>
<SCRIPT>
letter = "A"
while (letter != "q")
{
letter = prompt("Enter a character from the keyboard", " ")
if (letter < " ")
    alert("Non-printing character entered")
if (letter >= "a" && letter <= "z")
    alert("Lower case letter entered")
if (letter >= "A" && letter <= "Z")
    alert("Upper case letter entered")
if (letter >= "0" && letter <= "9")
    alert("Digit entered")
}
</SCRIPT>
</HTML>
```

The program keeps looping round until a 'q' is generated

So far, so good. This handles the non-printing characters (0 to 31) up to space, and the sets, 'a' to 'z', 'A' to 'Z' and '0' to '9'. Now what about the rest? Look at any character set (use Windows' Character Map), and you will see that there are punctuation and other symbols scattered between the blocks of letters and digits. A test for these would look like this – and I'm not guaranteeing that this is correct!:

```
if ((letter >= ' ') && (letter <= '0') || (letter >= '9') && (letter <= 'a') ||
    (letter >= '\') && (letter <= 'A') || (letter >= 'Z'))
```

96

Here's a better solution. The **if ... else** structure gives two branches from the same test – one to follow if it is true, and one if it is false. This can be extended to handle multiple branching.

```
if (test1)
    {statement(s) if test1 is true}
else if (test2)
    {statement(s) if test2 is true}
...
else
    {statement(s) if no tests are true}
```

If *test1* is false, the program tries *test2*, and failing that, tries the next. If all the tests prove false, the program performs the statements after the final **else**. Here's the revised character analysis routine.

chars2.htm

```
<HTML>
<HEAD>
<TITLE>Character testing2</TITLE>
</HEAD>
<BODY>
<SCRIPT>
letter = "A"
while (letter != "q")
{
letter = prompt("Enter a character from the keyboard", " ")
if (letter < " ")
    alert("Non-printing character entered")
else if (letter >= "a" && letter <= "z")
    alert("Lower case letter entered")
else if (letter >= "A" && letter <= "Z")
    alert("Upper case letter entered")
else if (letter >= "0" && letter <= "9")
    alert("Digit entered")
else
    alert("Symbol entered")
}
</SCRIPT>
</HTML>
```

If the flow reaches this point, the character is not non-printing, not a letter and not a digit

97

The conditional operator

JavaScript supports the conditional operator ? : which is a form of shorthand for **if ... else**. It can sometimes be convenient, though what you gain in compactness you lose in readability. Here's a simple example of its use:

```
admission = ( age < 18 ? 5 : 10)
```

This is equivalent to the structure:

```
if (age < 18)
    admission = 5
else
    admission = 10
```

It is more commonly used within a larger expression. For example, this firm charges £7.50 delivery for orders under £100. The line to calculate the amount due is:

```
cost = total + (total < 100 ? 7.5 : 0)
```

Using if ... else, the code would be:

```
if (total < 100)
    cost = total + 7.50
else
    cost = total
```

Which brings us to an alternative solution to the problem of spacing when laying out tables of figures. We can use ? : instead of resorting to the TABLE tags.

In the times table, which runs up to 6 x 10, the results can be 1 or 2 digits long. If we copy the output into a string, with 3 dots before the 1 digit values and 2 dots before the 2 digit values, the numbers should line up – or at least, they will if we use the Courier font, with its fixed character widths.

The key line in this program is:

```
output = (mult < 10 ? "..." : "..") + mult
```

If you wanted to extend the table to values over 99, the line would be:

```
output = (mult < 10 ? "..." : "..") + (mult < 100 ? "." : "") + mult
```

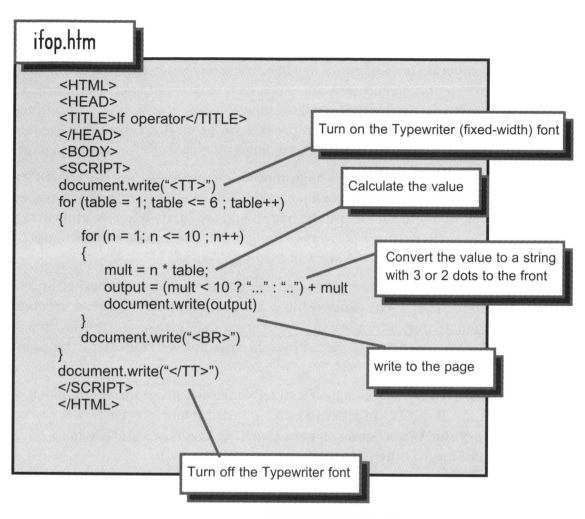

```
ifop.htm

<HTML>
<HEAD>
<TITLE>If operator</TITLE>
</HEAD>
<BODY>
<SCRIPT>
document.write("<TT>")                           Turn on the Typewriter (fixed-width) font
for (table = 1; table <= 6 ; table++)
{                                                Calculate the value
    for (n = 1; n <= 10 ; n++)
    {
        mult = n * table;                        Convert the value to a string
        output = (mult < 10 ? "..." : "..") + mult    with 3 or 2 dots to the front
        document.write(output)
    }
    document.write("<BR>")                       write to the page
}
document.write("</TT>")
</SCRIPT>
</HTML>

                                                 Turn off the Typewriter font
```

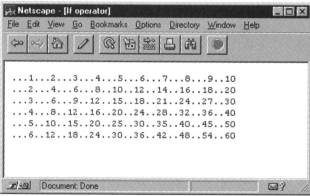

Using functions

A function is a self-contained block of code. It may carry out some kind of calculation and return a value, or it may simply perform a task. In most programming languages, functions (or the similar subroutines and methods) are used to break a program down into manageable chunks – it's hard to read and debug a block of code larger than a page.

In JavaScript, functions have another purpose. As they can be written into the <HEAD> area of a page, you can be sure that they are loaded and ready to run before the page begins to load. Where scripts are in the <BODY>, there is always a danger that the browser will attempt to run them while they are still loading.

A function is called (activated) by giving its name in another line of code. After it has been executed, the program flow returns to the code immediately after the call. The process can be taken further, with one function calling another. Program flow always returns to the point after the call.

Here's a trivial example. First, let's take the program as one block of code. It raises a number to a power, using a loop. To see how it works, 'dry run' the program on paper, writing down the values held by *temp* and *loop* as the program runs through the loop:

power1.htm

```
<HTML>
<HEAD>
<TITLE>Power in the body</TITLE>
</HEAD>
<BODY>
<SCRIPT>
num = 4;
p = 3;
temp = 1;
for (loop = 1; loop <= p; loop++)
          temp = temp * num;
     document.write(num + " to the power of " + p + " = " + temp)
</SCRIPT>
</HTML>
```

Use any values you like, but **p** should be an integer

Now let's try again using a function. In this version, both the calculation and the output lines have been transferred to the function.

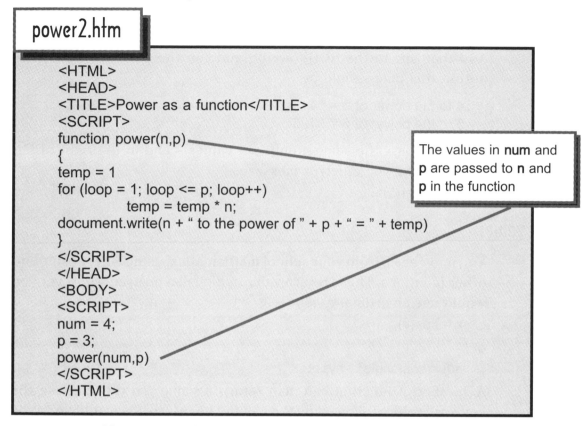

```
power2.htm

<HTML>
<HEAD>
<TITLE>Power as a function</TITLE>
<SCRIPT>
function power(n,p)
{
temp = 1
for (loop = 1; loop <= p; loop++)
          temp = temp * n;
document.write(n + " to the power of " + p + " = " + temp)
}
</SCRIPT>
</HEAD>
<BODY>
<SCRIPT>
num = 4;
p = 3;
power(num,p)
</SCRIPT>
</HTML>
```

The values in **num** and **p** are passed to **n** and **p** in the function

Notice its definition line:

```
function power(n,p)
```

The parameters **(n,p)** take two values from the calling line, and they act as normal variables within **power()**. **num** is passed to **n** in **power()**, and **p** in the BODY script is passed to **p** in **power()**.

The choice of names is deliberate – the names of parameters can be the same as or different from those of the variables that are passed to them. The parameters and variables in **power( )** are completely separate from those in the BODY script.

Parameters

When passing values to a method, you must pass the right type of data, though it can be either as a variable or a literal value. This call to **power()** would also work:

```
document.write("5 to the power of 5 = " + power(5,5))
```

Add that line to the BODY script, and run the program again. The output this time should be:

```
4 to the power of 3 = 64
5 to the power of 5 = 3125
```

You must pass the same number of values – and in the right order. This will give you an error message:

```
power(5);
```

Return values

You may recall, from your school mathematics, using Sine, Cosine and other functions. These return value, which can be used wherever you would use an ordinary value, e.g.

```
x = cos(y)
```

or

```
adj = cos(angle) * hypot
```

A JavaScript function can also return a value. To do this, use the keyword **return** followed by the value. The **return** line would normally be the last – or perhaps the only – line in the function. You might, for instance, define a function **cube()** like this:

```
function cube(x)
{
    return x * x * x
}
```

Here's the Power program again, this time rewritten so that the **power()** function returns the result to the calling code.

power3.htm

```
<HTML>
<HEAD>
<TITLE>Power as a function</TITLE>
<SCRIPT>
function power(n,p)
{
temp = 1
for (loop = 1; loop <= p; loop++)
        temp = temp * n;
return temp
}
</SCRIPT>
</HEAD>
<BODY>
<SCRIPT>
num = 4;
p = 3;
ans = power(num,p)
document.write(number + " to the power of " + p + " = " + ans)
</SCRIPT>
</HTML>
```

> The value in **temp** is returned to the calling code

> This calls **power()** and copies the returned value to **ans**

Notice the line that calls the function:

    ans = power(num,p)

A simple **power(num,p)** would not get the answer. Bearing in mind that a function that returns a value is treated as any other value, you could equally well call it from within the write line:

document.write(num + " to the power of " + p + " = " + **power(num,p)**)

A function can have several return lines. Here is a function, **compare()**, which tests two values and returns 1 if the first is larger, −1 if it is smaller or 0 if they are the same:

```
function compare(a,b)
        {
            if (a > b)  return 1
            else if (a < b)  return -1

            else return 0

        }
```

103

Exercises

1   Write a program, using two loops, to produce this pattern of asterisks:

```
*
**
***
****
*****
******
*******
********
*********
**********
```

2   Find out how fast JavaScript runs on your PC. Write a program that displays "Starting to count", runs through a loop, then displays "Done".

How long does it take your PC to count to 10,000? How long to count to 1,000,000?

Tip: Write "<P>" at the end of the first line. If you don't, the whole program will run before anything appears on the screen.

3   How random are the numbers produced by **random()**? Set up an array of 10 numbers, then generate random numbers in the range 0 to 9 and increment the matching element in the array. This should loop round for at least 1,000 times. Display the results at the end.

4   The factorial of a number is that number multiplied by every integer below it, down to one. For example, factorial 4 = 4 * 3 * 2 * 1 = 24. Write a function to calculate factorials, and set it in a page which asks the user for a number, then displays its factorial.

6 Active pages

Dates

If you want to do any work with dates or time, investigate the **Date( )** object. You can use it to:

● get the current date and time from your system's clock

● convert a date written in words and figures (or just figures) into a standard Date form

● extract or set any part of the date, from year down to second

● calculate elapsed time between two dates or times.

To create a Date object and set it to the current date and time, use:

```
today = new Date( )
```

To create a Date object for any other date, use one of these forms:

```
myParty = new Date("November 5th, 1997 19:30:00")
myParty  = new Date(1997, 11, 1, 19, 30, 0)
```

Where the date is written as text the whole expression must be enclosed in quotes. The last three figures – hours, minutes, seconds – are optional in both forms.

If you write the Date value or copy it to a text box, without processing it in any way, it will be displayed in this standard form:

```
Sat Sep 20 10:54:31 GMT Daylight Time 1997
```

This is clear, but not very attractive. Better displays need some work.

The methods **getYear()**, **getMonth()**, **getDay()**, **getDate()**, **getHours()**, **getMinutes( )**, and **getSeconds( )** will extract the relevant value – though as a number.

```
thisDay = today.getDay()
```

Gives me 6 just now – it's Saturday as I write this, and the week starts from 0 on Sunday.

If you want to display the month or day in words, you will have to set up arrays.

```
days = new Array("Sunday", "Monday", "Tuesday", "Wednesday",
"Thursday", "Friday", "Saturday")
```

days[thisDay] will now display "Saturday". Look for a version of this, and for a similar routine to handle months in the next example.

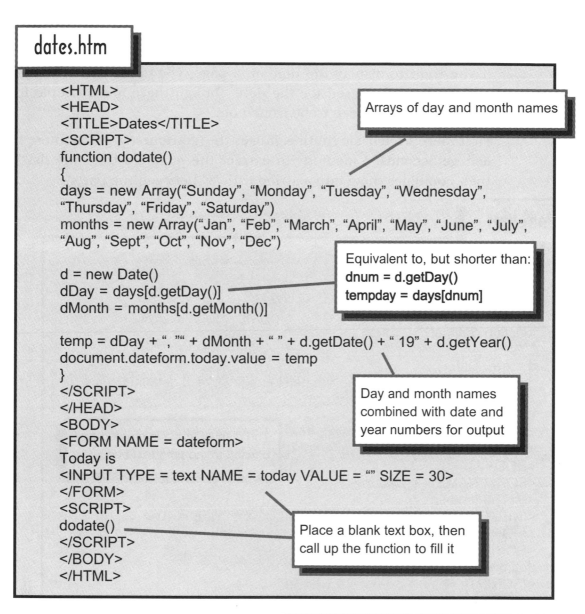

dates.htm

```
<HTML>
<HEAD>
<TITLE>Dates</TITLE>
<SCRIPT>
function dodate()
{
days = new Array("Sunday", "Monday", "Tuesday", "Wednesday",
"Thursday", "Friday", "Saturday")
months = new Array("Jan", "Feb", "March", "April", "May", "June", "July",
"Aug", "Sept", "Oct", "Nov", "Dec")

d = new Date()
dDay = days[d.getDay()]
dMonth = months[d.getMonth()]

temp = dDay + ", "" + dMonth + " " + d.getDate() + " 19" + d.getYear()
document.dateform.today.value = temp
}
</SCRIPT>
</HEAD>
<BODY>
<FORM NAME = dateform>
Today is
<INPUT TYPE = text NAME = today VALUE = "" SIZE = 30>
</FORM>
<SCRIPT>
dodate()
</SCRIPT>
</BODY>
</HTML>
```

Arrays of day and month names

Equivalent to, but shorter than:
dnum = d.getDay()
tempday = days[dnum]

Day and month names combined with date and year numbers for output

Place a blank text box, then call up the function to fill it

The new display is worth the effort!

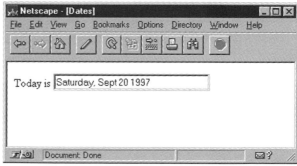

Today is | Saturday, Sept 20 1997

107

Time

If you want to display the time on a page, you could use a similar technique to that used for the date, though there are a couple fo wrinkles that will need to be ironed out.

First, here's the basic routine. It uses the **getHours()**, **getMinutes()**, and **getSeconds()** methods to extract the numbers from the date, then combines them into a string with ":" between the parts.

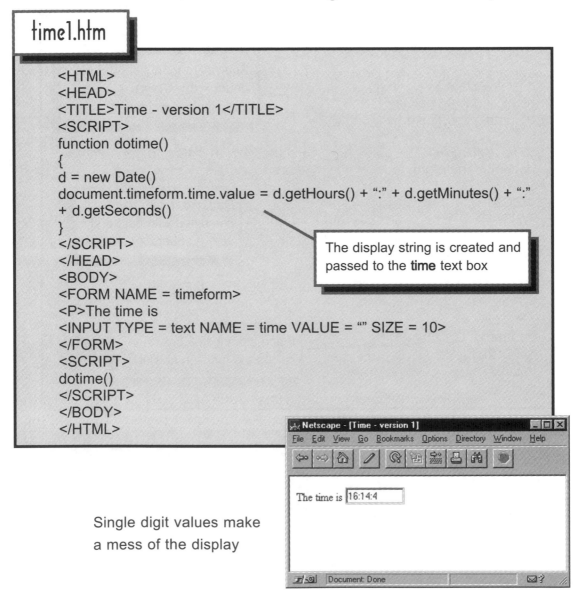

time1.htm

```
<HTML>
<HEAD>
<TITLE>Time - version 1</TITLE>
<SCRIPT>
function dotime()
{
d = new Date()
document.timeform.time.value = d.getHours() + ":" + d.getMinutes() + ":"
+ d.getSeconds()
}
</SCRIPT>
</HEAD>
<BODY>
<FORM NAME = timeform>
<P>The time is
<INPUT TYPE = text NAME = time VALUE = "" SIZE = 10>
</FORM>
<SCRIPT>
dotime()
</SCRIPT>
</BODY>
</HTML>
```

The display string is created and passed to the **time** text box

The time is 16:14:4

Single digit values make a mess of the display

108

Improving the display

The first problem with our simple routine is that single digit values do not look good. They would be improved by a leading '0'. Here is an ideal opportunity to use the conditional operator ? : that you met in Chapter 5. The expression:

    (d.getMinutes()<10) ? ":0" : ":"

will produce ":0" when the minutes are in single digits, and ":" otherwise. We can use this instead of a plain ":" when creating the output string – though note that the whole expression must be enclosed in brackets. Change the output line to read:

```
document.timeform.time.value = d.getHours() + ((d.getMinutes()<10) ? ":0" : ":")
+ d.getMinutes() + ((d.getSeconds()<10) ? ":0" : ":") + d.getSeconds()
```

It is not pretty, and you must make sure that all the opening and closing brackets are in the right places, but the resulting display is far better.

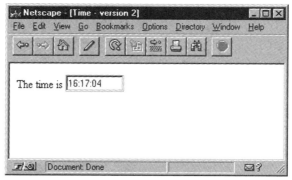

When is now?

The second problem is that your 'clock' will only be right when the page is first opened. It isn't going! If you want to show the right time all the time, the clock must be updated constantly – and for that we need Timeouts. Read on...

Timeout

Timeouts allow you to set a delay before a command is executed. At the simplest, you just give the **setTimeout()** method the job to do and the number of milliseconds to wait before doing it. For example

```
setTimeout("alert('You have been here 5 seconds')",5000)
```

Five seconds after the page has loaded, an alert will pop up. Notice those quotes around the command – they are crucial! If you miss them out, the command will be executed, but the delay will be ignored.

If you want the action repeated at regular intervals, the Timeout should be written into the action, setting it up for the next time.

```
function irritate()
{
    reply = confirm("Enjoying your visit?")
    if (reply == true)
        setTimeout("irritate()",5000)
}
```

Once this has been started, by an "irritate()" somewhere in the main script, it will run every five seconds until the visitor clicks 'Cancel'.

If you want to be able to stop the repetition, either make the call dependent on a test, as above, or use the **clearTimeout()** method. This needs to know which Timeout to clear – there can be any number running at once – so the **setTimeout()** must be created in a slightly different form, giving it a name.

```
timer1 = setTimeout("alert('Have a nice day')", 10000)
...
clearTimeout(timer1)
```

The next example puts a mock 'visitor counter' on the page, updating it constantly – set the delay to reflect your page's popularity!

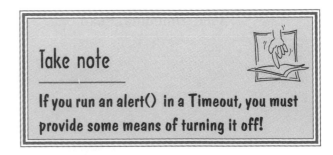

Take note

If you run an alert() in a Timeout, you must provide some means of turning it off!

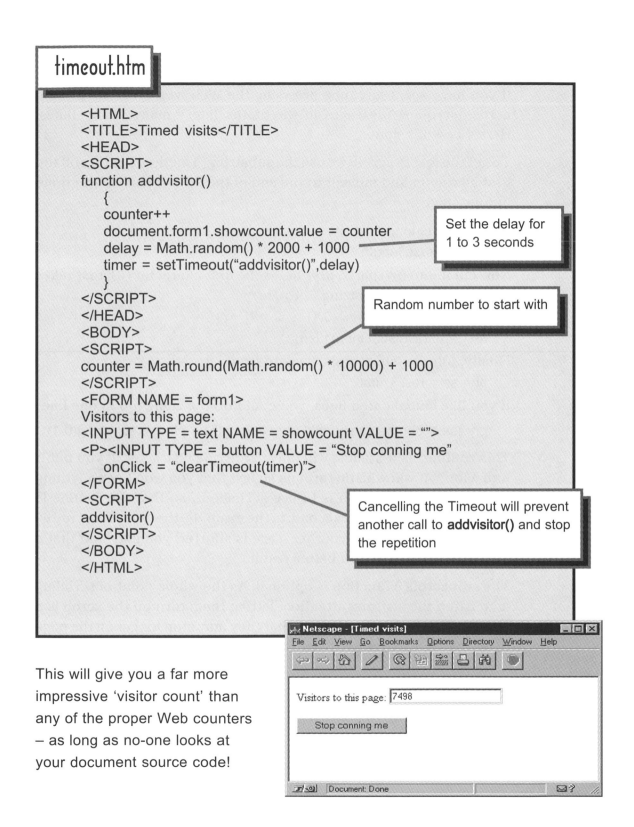

timeout.htm

```html
<HTML>
<TITLE>Timed visits</TITLE>
<HEAD>
<SCRIPT>
function addvisitor()
    {
    counter++
    document.form1.showcount.value = counter
    delay = Math.random() * 2000 + 1000
    timer = setTimeout("addvisitor()",delay)
    }
</SCRIPT>
</HEAD>
<BODY>
<SCRIPT>
counter = Math.round(Math.random() * 10000) + 1000
</SCRIPT>
<FORM NAME = form1>
Visitors to this page:
<INPUT TYPE = text NAME = showcount VALUE = "">
<P><INPUT TYPE = button VALUE = "Stop conning me"
    onClick = "clearTimeout(timer)">
</FORM>
<SCRIPT>
addvisitor()
</SCRIPT>
</BODY>
</HTML>
```

Set the delay for 1 to 3 seconds

Random number to start with

Cancelling the Timeout will prevent another call to **addvisitor()** and stop the repetition

This will give you a far more impressive 'visitor count' than any of the proper Web counters – as long as no-one looks at your document source code!

Netscape - [Timed visits]

File   Edit   View   Go   Bookmarks   Options   Directory   Window   Help

Visitors to this page: 7498

Stop conning me

Document: Done

Scrolling text

If you have spent any time browsing the Web, you must have come across scrolling messages in the Status line – many, many times! Here's how it's done.

To get the text to scroll, we use the **substring()** method to chop off the first character and move it to the end of the string. This is best done in four stages.

First find the length of the string:

```
len = phrase.length
```

Now cut it into two parts: *first* holds the first character (0); *rest* takes the remainder of the string (1 to *len*)

```
first = phrase.substring(0,1)
rest = phrase.substring(1,len)
```

Finally, join the substrings, back to front.

```
phrase = rest + first
```

If you like complicated lines, you could do the same job in one line:

```
phrase = phrase.substring(1,phrase.length) + phrase.substring(0,1)
```

This routine, as it stands, will only scroll one character. If you put it into a loop, it will whistle through so fast that you won't see anything happening. The solution is to use a Timeout, so that the routine is executed several times a second. In the example, the delay is set to 100 – 1/10th of a second. If your message is shorter, you may find that a longer delay produces a better result.

The **stopscroll()** function is optional. As the whole point of scrolling is to catch the visitors' attention, letting them turn off the scroll is a bit counter-productive – except that they may stop longer on the page once the distraction has been removed!

scroller.htm

```
<HTML>
<HEAD>
<TITLE>Scroller</TITLE>
<SCRIPT>
function setstatus()
{
    len = phrase.length
    first = phrase.substring(0,1)
    rest = phrase.substring(1,len)
    phrase = rest + first
    self.status = phrase
    timerID = setTimeout("setstatus()",100)
}
function stopscroll()
{
    clearTimeout(timerID)
    self.status = 'Now I shall sulk'
}
</SCRIPT>
</HEAD>
<BODY>
<FORM>
<INPUT TYPE = button VALUE = "Stop that irritating scroll!"
    onClick = "stopscroll()">
</FORM>
<SCRIPT>
phrase = new String("...Made Simples are good for you...Go out and buy
one now...")
setstatus()
</SCRIPT>
</BODY>
</HTML>
```

Move the first character to the end of the string and pass it to the Status line

Replace or rewrite the Status message

Allocate the message to a new **String** object

Netscape - [Scroller]

File Edit View Go Bookmarks Options Directory Window Help

Stop that irritating scroll!

d buy one now......Made Simples are good

Sounds

JavaScript, on its own, does not have any means of handling sounds. However, it can use the facilities of LiveAudio, one of the the standard plugins.

If you want to simply play a sound, as soon as it is loaded, and without giving your visitors any say in the matter, then you can do it from straight HTML. This simple line will load and play a sound file:

```
<EMBED SRC= "background.mid" HIDDEN=TRUE>
```

The **HIDDEN=TRUE** clause is not strictly necessary, but if you omit it, part of the sound player will be displayed on screen.

Sound file formats

LiveAudio can handle sounds in four formats:

AU   Developed by Sun, and the only format that Java can handle

AIFF   The Apple format

WAV   Native to Windows – any sounds you save with the Sound Recorder will be in this format

MIDI   The standard for digital music.

If you are working on a PC and have a microphone, you can easily record your own WAV (Waveform) files, but do note that they tend to be large. A second of WAV sound takes anything from 8Kb to 172Kb depending on the quality – the standard WAV takes 22Kb per second. This is because Waveform files are made by 'sampling' sound thousands of times each second, converting the sound wave to a digital value. If you are tempted to record a "Hello and welcome to all my visitors" message for your page, be aware that your visitors may have got bored and left before the file has downloaded!

If you want background music, you need suitable music software and/ or a keyboard to create MIDI files. They store music far more compactly, by defining each note in terms of the type of instrument, length, pitch and volume. As a result, a 20Kb MIDI file will give you a couple of minutes, or more, of multi-track music. If you can't create your own, hunt on the Internet for (copyright-free!) ones.

Controlling sound

LiveAudio, and JavaScript's LiveConnect links give you a number of methods for controlling sound files. These are the key ones:

play(*loop*)   starts to play the sound. The *loop* setting can be *true*, *false* or number of times you want to repeat it.

pause( )   halts playing when first called, and restarts next time. **play( )** will also restart it.

stop( )   stops the selected file playing.

StopAll( )   stops all current sound files – this is irrelevant with WAV files, which can only be played one at a time.

GetVolume( )   returns the volume level as a percentage.

setvol(num)   sets the volume to a new percentage level.

IsReady( )   returns *true* if the file is fully loaded.

As with any other methods, **play( )**, **pause( )** and **stop( )** must be related to an object, which means that you have to identify the sound file. The most reliable way to do this is to give it a name, and this must be accompanied by the keyword MASTERSOUND. For example:

```
<EMBED SRC= "mySound.wav" HIDDEN=TRUE AUTOSTART=FALSE
  NAME= "mySound" MASTERSOUND>
```

Notice the **AUTOSTART=FALSE** clause, so that the sound does not begin to play automatically.

To start the sound, and play it once only, we can use a line such as:

```
document.mySound.play(false)
```

To turn the volume up by 10%, we can use code like this:

```
vol = document.mySound.GetVolume() + 10
if (vol < 100)
    document.mySound.setvol(vol)
```

Take note

The volume controls do not work with some sound cards and drivers.

```
<HTML>
<HEAD>
<SCRIPT>
function playSound()
{
    document.mySound.play(false)
}
function pauseSound()
{
  document.mySound.pause()
}
function stopSound()
{
  document.mySound.stop()
}
function louder()
{
  vol = document.mySound.GetVolume()+ 10
  if (vol <= 100)
    document.mySound.setvol(vol)
}
function quieter()
{
  vol = document.mySound.GetVolume()- 10
  if (vol >= 0 )
    document.mySound.setvol(vol)
}
</SCRIPT>
</HEAD>
<BODY>
<EMBED SRC= "mySound.wav" HIDDEN=TRUE AUTOSTART=FALSE
  NAME= "mySound" MASTERSOUND>
<FORM>
<INPUT TYPE = button VALUE = " Play " onClick= "playSound()">
<INPUT TYPE = button VALUE = " Pause " onClick= "pauseSound()">
<INPUT TYPE = button VALUE = " Stop " onClick= "stopSound()">
<INPUT TYPE = button VALUE = " Louder " onClick= "louder()">
<INPUT TYPE = button VALUE = " Quieter " onClick= "quieter()">
</BODY>
</HTML>
```

These commands could have been written directly into the onClick = ...

Check the 0 and 100 limits

Buttons are the simplest way to give your visitors control

116

The embeds array

From Netscape 3.0 onwards, the system automatically forms the EMBED objects into an array called *embeds[]*. This can offer a very convenient way of handling sets of sound files, as long as you don't mind the fact that users of older browsers won't be able to hear them!

If you are going to use the embeds[] array, you do not need to bother about naming the sound files. You should, however, continue to hide them, and turn off the Autostart. A suitable EMBED line would be:

```
<EMBED SRC= "chord.wav" HIDDEN=TRUE AUTOSTART=FALSE>
```

The EMBED objects are added to the array in the order that they appear in the page source, with the first numbered as *embeds[0]*. Thus, to play the third file, you would use:

```
document.embeds[2].play(false)
```

The subscript can, of course, be a variable, and this is what makes the array so useful. By passing the subscript as a parameter, you can make one function play any sound on the page:

```
<INPUT TYPE = button VALUE = " F " onClick= "playSound(4)">
...
function playSound(num)
{
    document.embeds[num].play(false)
}
```

You can create a routine to play a sequence of sounds. A simple loop will not work for this, as each new **play( )** instruction will stop the previous sound, and do it so quickly that it won't get a chance to start! The solution is to use a Timeout, allowing sufficient delay between each. Here's the scale-playing routine from the next example.

```
note = 0
function playScale()
{
    document.embeds[note].play(false)
    note++
    if (note < 9)
        setTimeout("playScale()",500)
}
```

The variable *note* is set to 0 when the function is first called, then incremented before the next call. An apparently neater solution is to pass the subscript as a parameter like this:

```
function playScale(note)
{
document.embeds[note].play(false)
    note++
    if (note < 9)
        setTimeout("playScale(note)",500)
}
```

Unfortuately, that will not work. When the Timeout calls playScale(), it gives an error, saying that 'note is not defined'. I'm still trying to fathom why!

To be able to run the next example, you will need a set of sound files, each of which will play a separate note. Record your own, if you can. And if you can't, there is an octave of notes available on-line at:

http://www.tcp.co.uk/~macbride/javasound.htm

sounds2.htm

```
<HTML>
<HEAD>
<SCRIPT>
function playSound(num)
{
document.embeds[num].play(false)
}

note = 0
function playScale()
{
document.embeds[note].play(false)
    note++
    if (note < 9)
        setTimeout("playScale()",500)
}
</SCRIPT>
</HEAD>
```

Plays any EMBED sound, once

Works through, stopping at **embeds[8]**

Create your own sound files, or use mine

```
<BODY>
<EMBED SRC= "chord.wav" HIDDEN=TRUE AUTOSTART=FALSE>
<EMBED SRC= "cnote.wav" HIDDEN=TRUE AUTOSTART=FALSE>
<EMBED SRC= "dnote.wav" HIDDEN=TRUE AUTOSTART=FALSE>
<EMBED SRC= "enote.wav" HIDDEN=TRUE AUTOSTART=FALSE>
<EMBED SRC= "fnote.wav" HIDDEN=TRUE AUTOSTART=FALSE>
<EMBED SRC= "gnote.wav" HIDDEN=TRUE AUTOSTART=FALSE>
<EMBED SRC= "anote.wav" HIDDEN=TRUE AUTOSTART=FALSE>
<EMBED SRC= "bnote.wav" HIDDEN=TRUE AUTOSTART=FALSE>
<EMBED SRC= "ctop.wav" HIDDEN=TRUE AUTOSTART=FALSE>

<FORM>
<INPUT TYPE = button VALUE = "C major" onClick= "playSound(0)">
<P>
<INPUT TYPE = button VALUE = " C " onClick= "playSound(1)">
<INPUT TYPE = button VALUE = " D " onClick= "playSound(2)">
<INPUT TYPE = button VALUE = " E " onClick= "playSound(3)">
<INPUT TYPE = button VALUE = " F " onClick= "playSound(4)">
<INPUT TYPE = button VALUE = " G " onClick= "playSound(5)">
<INPUT TYPE = button VALUE = " A " onClick= "playSound(6)">
<INPUT TYPE = button VALUE = " B " onClick= "playSound(7)">
<INPUT TYPE = button VALUE = " C " onClick= "playSound(8)">
<P>
<INPUT TYPE = button VALUE = "Play the scale"
   onClick= "note = 1; playScale()">
</FORM>
</BODY>
</HTML>
```

It's hardly hi-tech HiFi, but the possibilities are there if you care to put in the time and effort

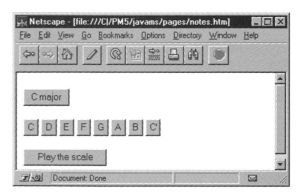

119

Exercises

1   Write a routine to calculate and display the number of days between when your page was last updated and when it is viewed in the browser.

2   Use a Timeout to calculate and display the amount of time that a page has been opened. This can be shown in seconds, or in minutes and seconds.

3   Combine the solution from exercise 2 with the example on page 108 to show your visitors' time of arrival and the amount of time they have spent there.

4   Set up a form containing a text box and a button. Design and write a script that will allow the button to start and stop a message scrolling in the text box.

   Tip: You will need a boolean (true/false) variable to flag whether the scrolling is turned on or off.

7 Working with images

Image files

Web browsers – and therefore JavaScript – can only handle graphics files in two formats – GIF (including animated GIFs) and JPEG (with either a .JPEG or a .JPG extension). The standard Windows formats BMP and PCX cannot be used. If you want to create your own images, you will need a suitable graphics application, such as Paint Shop Pro. You can use this for drawing new images, or for converting pictures created in Paint – or anywhere else – into the GIF or JPEG formats.

As a general rule, you should use the GIF format in preference to JPEG. GIF files are significantly smaller, and therefore faster to load – an important consideration, especially where files have to be transferred over the World Wide Web. The main reason why JPEG files are larger is that they have palettes of 16.7 million colours, as opposed to the 256-colour palette of GIFs. Use JPEGs only where you need to show subtle variations of colour over a huge palette – and if the file is going up onto the Web, remember that many people will be viewing it on 256, or even 16-colour screens!

An animated GIF is a set of images, which are displayed in sequence, with a defined delay between each. They are used in exactly the same way as still images – the animation is entirely built into the image file, so all Java has to do is display it. The main things to remember here are that the files tend to be large, and that the animation speed is defined within the GIF. There are plenty of ready-made animated GIFs freely available on the Web – dig around in any shareware site and you should find lots – and if you want to create your own, go to Microsoft's site and pick up a copy of GIF Animator.

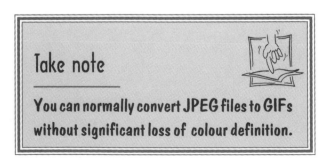

Take note

You can normally convert JPEG files to GIFs without significant loss of colour definition.

Image objects

Images can be created in two ways – with the **<IMG>** tag and with the **Image( )** constructor.

<IMG> images are, of course, placed on the form and have a whole set of properties that can be used to format their position, size and appearance. The images are automatically formed into the array *images[ ]*, and numbered in the order of their position in the document. So the first image can be referred to as *document.images[0]*.

Image( ) images exist only in cache (temporary) memory. They allow you to preload images for later display and are especially useful in animation and other situations where you want to be able to drop in a new image without downloading delay.

```
storedImage = new Image()
storedImage.src = "newpic.gif"

tinyImage = new Image(50,25)
tinyImage.src = "newpic.gif"
```

These lines set up two Image( ) objects, *storedImage* and *tinyImage*, both holding the same picture. *storedImage* holds the picture at its original size. When *tinyImage* was set up, the optional width and height parameters were set, so that it holds the image in a reduced form, 50 pixels wide and 25 pixels high.

Image( ) objects have a smaller set of properties, and the most important is probably *complete*. This is set to *true* if the image has been fully downloaded.

Unlike <IMG>s, Image( ) objects are not automatically put into an array, which is a bit of a shame because you often need them in one. To set up an array, first load the images into separate objects, then create a new array, giving it the names of the objects.

```
pic0 = new Image()
pic0.src = "reddart.gif"
pic1 = new Image()
pic1.src = "bluedart.gif"
pic2 = new Image()
...
picA = new Array(pic0,pic1,pic2,pic3)
```

Simple animation

There's one big restriction on the amount of animation that you can do in JavaScript – you cannot change the position of images on the page, once the page has been loaded. However, you can change the picture held in an <IMG>, and that's how you can get your animation.

In the next example, four coloured darts 'move' right to left in a continuous loop. (It can easily be extended across the width of the page, but this demonstrates the technique – if you want to do the extra typing, you're welcome.) The core of the code is in these few lines:

```
for (loop = 0; loop < 4; loop++)
{
    index = (index < 3) ? ++index : 0
    document.images[index].src = picA[loop].src
}
index--
```

index identifies the elements in the *images[]* array; *loop* identifies those in the *picA[]* array of images. Thus, the line:

```
document.images[index].src = picA[loop].src
```

copies an image from the stored array to the screen display, and as it runs through the loop, all four are copied onto the screen. We have to write the routine so that, each time the function is called, the images are copied into different places.

```
index = (index < 3) ? ++index : 0
```

Increments the index as long as it is less than 3, and otherwise rests it to 0 – in effect, it takes it in turn through the values 0, 1, 2, 3, then back to 0. Writing **index--** at the end of the routine makes sure that, next time round, the index starts at a new value.

Notice the first two lines of **animate( )**:

```
if (going)
    clearTimeout(timer)
```

If you miss these out, then pressing the 'Roll em' button, while the animation is running, will start it off again. It will set up a second (or a third or more) Timeout that will also execute the *animate()* function. The result will be that the animation will run faster – and it will take the same number of 'Stop' presses to bring it to a complete halt.

The *checkload( )* function won't appear to do anything while you are testing the page on your system, but will be useful when you upload it to your Web space. By checking the complete property of the last of the image files, it will stop the page being displayed before all the images are ready for the animation.

animate.htm

```
<HTML>
<HEAD>
  <TITLE>Animating images </TITLE>
  <SCRIPT>
  function loadImages()
  {
    pic0 = new Image()
    pic0.src = "reddart.gif"
    pic1 = new Image()
    pic1.src = "bluedart.gif"
    pic2 = new Image()
    pic2.src = "grndart.gif"
    pic3 = new Image()
    pic3.src = "yelldart.gif"
    picA = new Array(pic0,pic1,pic2,pic3)
  }

  function animate()
  {
  if (going)
      clearTimeout(timer)

      for (loop = 0; loop < 4; loop++)
      {
        index = (index < 3) ? ++index : 0
        document.images[index].src = picA[loop].src
      }
      index--
      timer = setTimeout("animate()",200)
  }
```

Load images individually, then link them into the array **picA[]**

The Image() **src** property is the equivalent of IMG **SRC** in HTML

Stop the current Timeout, if one is running

Run the function again in 1/5th of a second

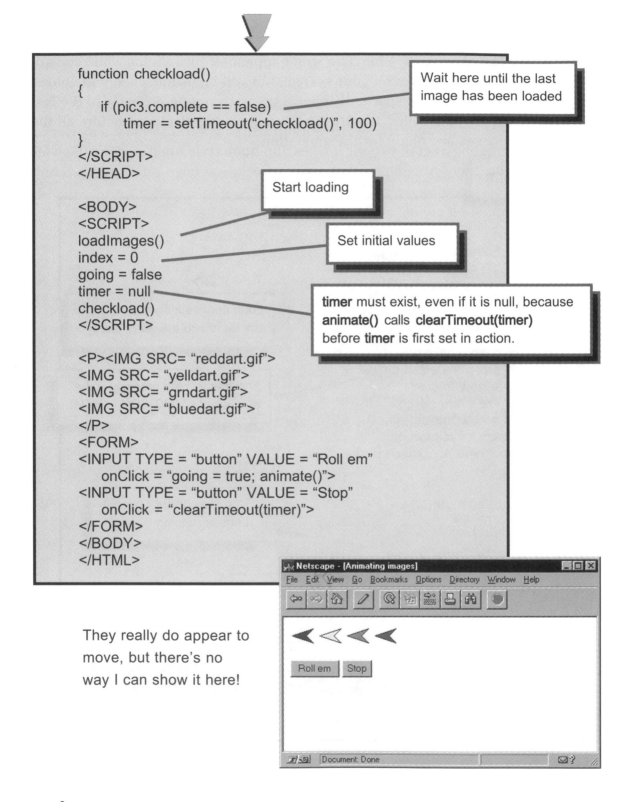

```
function checkload()
{
    if (pic3.complete == false)
        timer = setTimeout("checkload()", 100)
}
</SCRIPT>
</HEAD>

<BODY>
<SCRIPT>
loadImages()
index = 0
going = false
timer = null
checkload()
</SCRIPT>

<P><IMG SRC= "reddart.gif">
<IMG SRC= "yelldart.gif">
<IMG SRC= "grndart.gif">
<IMG SRC= "bluedart.gif">
</P>
<FORM>
<INPUT TYPE = "button" VALUE = "Roll em"
    onClick = "going = true; animate()">
<INPUT TYPE = "button" VALUE = "Stop"
    onClick = "clearTimeout(timer)">
</FORM>
</BODY>
</HTML>
```

Wait here until the last image has been loaded

Start loading

Set initial values

timer must exist, even if it is null, because **animate()** calls **clearTimeout(timer)** before **timer** is first set in action.

Netscape - [Animating images]
File Edit View Go Bookmarks Options Directory Window Help

Roll em   Stop

Document: Done

They really do appear to move, but there's no way I can show it here!

126

Animated GIFs

You don't need JavaScript to put animated GIFs on a page – just use a standard <IMG> tag. I am touching on them here because an animated GIF can be a neater solution to animation than a JavaScript routine.

Making an animated GIF is not difficult. It is basically just a matter of creating a set of varying images, flip-book style, then sticking them all together – though, as with any artwork, you need skill to get a really good-looking result. If you are not aiming for great art, all it takes is time and suitable software, such as *Microsoft GIF animator*.

1 Start by creating the images – all the same size, and with numbers in the names so that the order is clear.

2 Run the GIF animator and open the **last** of the set.

3 Use the **Insert** tool to add the other images, in reverse order – they are inserted before the current one.

4 On the **Image** tab, select each one in turn and and set its Duration.

5 On the **Animation** tab, turn on **Looping** and set the **Repeat** level.

6 Run the preview, and adjust the **Durations** if necessary.

7 Use Save As and save the file. That's it!

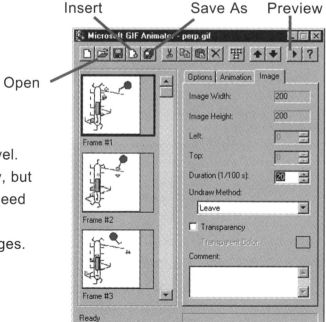

Insert   Save As   Preview

Open

There is no correct duration level. At 20/100 movements are jerky, but with lower durations you may need more intermediate images to achieve the same overall changes.

Animating GIFs

An animated GIF will always run at the same speed, for the same number of times – or forever. If you want to give your visitors some control over what happens and when, you need JavaScript. The demonstration program below uses one animated GIF and the set of individual GIFs from which it was made. Use your own, changing the names to suit, or download copies of mine from the demo page at:

http:/www.tcp.co.uk/~macbride/animation.htm

Five buttons give the visitor control of the images. They can be cycled through, backwards or forwards one at a time, or the animation run at speed, either forward or reverse.

Changing images is simpler than in the moving darts example, as only one <IMG> object is used. Here's the function that moves to the next image forward or back, depending on the value of *move* (1 or –1).

```
function nextpic()
{
    count+= move
    if (count<0)
        count = 5
    if (count> 5)
        count = 0
    document.motion.src = picArray[count].src
}
```

To get continual motion, all we need to do is set a Timeout, and call up *nextpic()*.

```
function animate()
{
    if (going)
        clearTimeout(timer)
    nextpic()
    timer = setTimeout("animate()",100)
}
```

To start it off, we just need to set *going* to true, assign a value to *move*, and call *animate( )* for the first time.

```
<INPUT TYPE = button VALUE = " Run "
    onClick = "going = true; move = 1; animate()">
```

```
<HTML>
<HEAD>
<SCRIPT>
{
    pic0 = new Image()
    pic0.src = "pic0.gif"
    pic1 = new Image()
    pic1.src = "pic1.gif"
    pic2 = new Image()
    pic2.src = "pic2.gif"
    pic3 = new Image()
    pic3.src = "pic3.gif"
    pic4 = new Image()
    pic4.src = "pic4.gif"
    pic5 = new Image()
    pic5.src = "pic5.gif"
picArray = new Array(pic0, pic1, pic2, pic3, pic4, pic5)
}
count = 0
function nextpic()
{
    count+= move
    if (count<0)
        count = 5
    if (count> 5)
        count = 0
    document.motion.src = picArray[count].src
}
timer = null
going = false
move = 1
 function animate()
    {
    if (going)
        clearTimeout(timer)
nextpic()
        timer = setTimeout("animate()",100)
    }
</SCRIPT>
</HEAD>
```

The array of images is set up as in animate.htm (page 125). Change the filenames if necessary

move will be 1 or –1

Delay set to 1/10th of a second – change to suit your images

129

```
<BODY>
<H3>Perpetual motion?</H3>
<IMG SRC = "perp.gif">This is an animated GIF
<IMG NAME = motion SRC = pic0.gif>This can be animated!
<FORM>
<INPUT TYPE = button VALUE = " Reverse "
    onClick = "going = true; move = -1; animate()">
<INPUT TYPE = button VALUE = " Back "
    onClick = "move = -1; nextpic()">
<INPUT TYPE = button VALUE = " Stop "
    onClick = "clearTimeout(timer)">
<INPUT TYPE = button VALUE = " Next "
    onClick = "move = 1; nextpic()">
<INPUT TYPE = button VALUE = " Run "
    onClick = "going = true; move = 1; animate()">
</FORM>
</BODY>
</HTML>
```

Instead or using **move** and a dual-purpose **nextpic()**, you could have separate functions for each button

This is my perpetual motion machine – and the animated GIF certainly runs perpetually without any prompting!

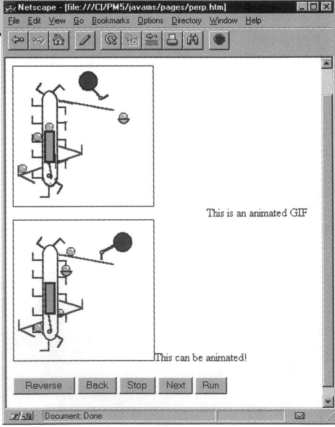

Image maps

The first job is to define the graphic for the image map. The graphic can be a photograph, scanned or painted picture; an integrated design or a collection of small images. Just keep its purpose in mind, and work towards that. Your visitors should be able to identify easily where they should click and what will happen when they click there.

The graphic is placed on the page with the <IMG SRC ...> tag, but using the option USEMAP = giving the image map's name. This could be based on the filename, but must be a single word and start with #.

    <IMG SRC = "imap.gif" USEMAP = "#imagemap">

This name is picked up again at the start of the mapping section. This is marked by the <MAP NAME = ...> tag.

    <MAP NAME = imagemap>

Note that the # is omitted here.The use of # in map names reflects its use in the names of anchors (see Chapter 2).

Each area of the map which is to carry a link is defined like this:

<AREA NAME= "spain" SHAPE= circle COORDS= "350,250,100" HREF = "spain.htm" onMouseOver= "window.status='Viva Espana'; return true">

<AREA   marks the start of the tag;

SHAPE =   is either *rect*, *circle*, *polygon* or *default*

COORDS = are the co-ordinates that define the shape.

    for *rect*, give the top left and bottom right corners, e.g.
        COORDS = "150,200,250,320"

    for *circle* give the centre, followed by the radius, e.g.
        COORDS="750,340,120"

    for *polygon*, give the x,y co-ordinates of each point, e.g.
        COORDS = 100, 100, 200, 100, 150, 50, 100, 100

    default is used to refer to the remainder of the graphic. You can also link a page to here, or if you do not want this to be 'clickable', set it to NOHREF.

HREF = ...> the URL of the page to be linked to the area.

onMouse... is where your JavaScript goes

Code for image maps

There are two event handlers that can be used on image maps – or on any other links.

onMouseOver=   when the cursor is on the area

onMouseOut=   when the cursor moves away

The most obvious use is for code to set the Status line message – this would replace the 'http://www...' which is usually shown when you are on a link.

onMouseOver= "window.status='Viva Espana'; return true"

And remember that **status=** in an event handler must be followed by **return true**.

But status line messages are not very visible. A clearer solution is to add a blank text box to the page, and output your message there.

onMouseOver="document.form1.message.value = 'Go to Opentext' "

A status line message is automatically replaced by the default status when the cursor moves off the area. If you are using a text box, you will need to attach some clearing code to **onMouseOut**.

In the example, the rectangle's Mouse events are both handled by functions – just to show that you can. The code could equally well have been written into the AREA tag.

imagemap.htm

```
<HTML>
<HEAD>
<TITLE>Image map</TITLE>
<SCRIPT>
function france()
{
    document.form1.message.value = "La belle France"
}
function blank()
{
    document.form1.message.value = ""
}
</SCRIPT>
</HEAD>
```

```
<BODY>
<SCRIPT>
window.defaultStatus= "blank"
</SCRIPT>
<IMG SRC = "immap.gif" USEMAP = "#imagemap">
<MAP NAME= "imagemap">
<AREA NAME= "france" SHAPE= rect COORDS="150,200,250,320"
   HREF = "france.htm" onMouseOver= "france()" onMouseOut = "blank()">
<AREA NAME= "spain" SHAPE= circle COORDS= "350,250,100"
    HREF = "spain.htm" onMouseOver= "window.status='Viva Espana'; return true">
<AREA NAME= "uk" SHAPE= polygon COORDS= "180,30,115,170,210,180,180,30"
   HREF = "" onMouseOver= "window.status= 'link not yet ready'; return true">
</MAP>
<FORM NAME = form1>
<INPUT TYPE = text NAME = message SIZE = 40>
</FORM>
</BODY>
</HTML>
```

onMouseOver won't work
without an HREF

End of the <MAP...>
section

The areas have been outlined
for this example, but would not
normally be visibly marked out.

Using a text box for the
message means that the
URL can be displayed in
the Status line as usual

133

Exercises

1   Design and write a routine that will appear to move an image across the page. As you cannot actually move images, you will need a set of IMG images into which the picture will be dropped. They will need to be filled initially with blank GIFs of the same size.

The animation example will serve as a starting point.

2   Start from the second animation example (page 127). Add two extra buttons, and adapt the code as necessary, so that the visitor can make the animation run faster or slower.

8 Interactive systems

Checkboxes and Radios

Back in Chapter 2 we looked at Checkboxes and Radio buttons as plain HTML tags, with the settings fed back via e-mail. There the feedback from Checkboxes was in the form of *name = on* (or *off*), while that from Radio buttons was in the form *name = value*. JavaScript won't give us these, but it does give us a number of different ways in which we can find the option settings.

First, let's see how we can identify Checkboxes and Radio buttons from within JavaScript.

- Checkboxes can be recognised, as normal, by NAME:
    document.form1.resources.

- Radio buttons, having only one NAME per set, are formed into arrays, numbered in order of their appearance:
    document.form1.mlist[0]

    The VALUE is irrelevant to JavaScript – only the position matters.

The checked property

Checkboxes and Radio buttons have a **checked** property, which is *true* when they are selected. We can test the *resources* Checkbox with:
    if (document.form1.resources.checked == true)

The test works just as well if you omit ==**true**
    if (document.form1.resources.checked)

The same approach works for Radio buttons:
    if (document.form1.mlist[0].checked)

If you are going to check an option more than once, or in complex expressions, you will get neater and more readable code by linking the option to a variable. This can be set by the **onClick** event.

Now you cannot do a simple:
    onClick = "software = true"

Checkboxes and Radio buttons are *toggles* – clicking them switches their state between *on* or *off*. You must test the **checked** property.
    onClick = "software = (this.checked ? true : false)"> Software sites

this refers to the current object – the Checkbox. **this.checked** will return true if the Checkbox is selected, and the ? : conditional test will set software to true or false accordingly.

You can simplify the expression by just copying the value of **checked** into the variable:

onClick = "software = this.checked"> Software sites

The next example shows all of these approaches in use. Notice that the **Submit** button has been replaced by one labelled 'Action', which calls up the *process()* function. If you want the feedback e-mailed to you, it is simper to stick to standard HTML. Use JavaScript when you want to find out information so that you can respond to your visitors while they are on-line. Here, all that happens is that alert boxes show the settings. In practice, you might use the selections to determine which page to display next, or what to write on that page.

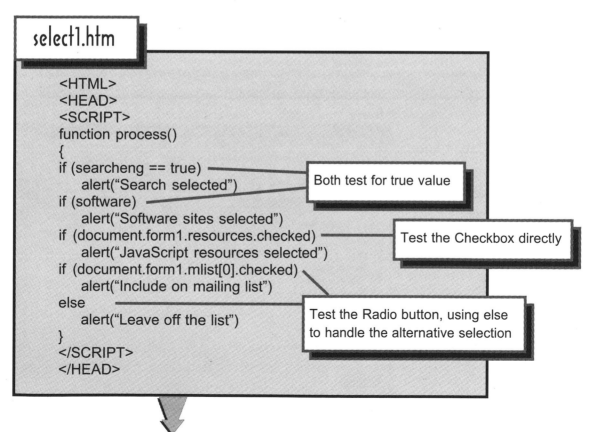

select1.htm

```
<HTML>
<HEAD>
<SCRIPT>
function process()
{
if (searcheng == true)
      alert("Search selected")
if (software)
      alert("Software sites selected")
if (document.form1.resources.checked)
      alert("JavaScript resources selected")
if (document.form1.mlist[0].checked)
      alert("Include on mailing list")
else
      alert("Leave off the list")
}
</SCRIPT>
</HEAD>
```

Both test for true value

Test the Checkbox directly

Test the Radio button, using else to handle the alternative selection

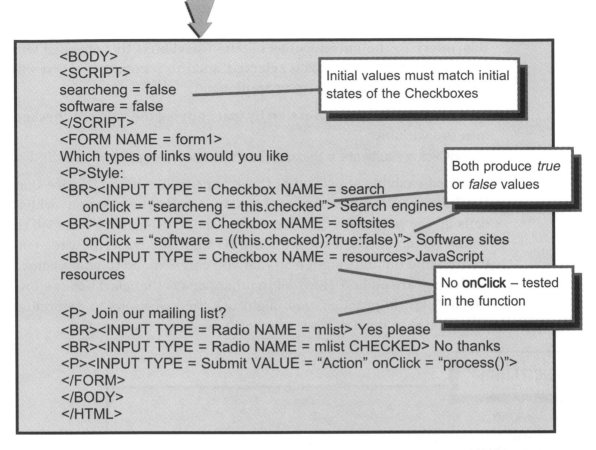

```
<BODY>
<SCRIPT>
searcheng = false
software = false
</SCRIPT>
<FORM NAME = form1>
Which types of links would you like
<P>Style:
<BR><INPUT TYPE = Checkbox NAME = search
    onClick = "searcheng = this.checked"> Search engines
<BR><INPUT TYPE = Checkbox NAME = softsites
    onClick = "software = ((this.checked)?true:false)"> Software sites
<BR><INPUT TYPE = Checkbox NAME = resources>JavaScript
resources

<P> Join our mailing list?
<BR><INPUT TYPE = Radio NAME = mlist> Yes please
<BR><INPUT TYPE = Radio NAME = mlist CHECKED> No thanks
<P><INPUT TYPE = Submit VALUE = "Action" onClick = "process()">
</FORM>
</BODY>
</HTML>
```

Initial values must match initial states of the Checkboxes

Both produce *true* or *false* values

No **onClick** – tested in the function

Look at the location line. After the Action button has been clicked, this shows the previous settings of the options – in the standard HTML feedback format.

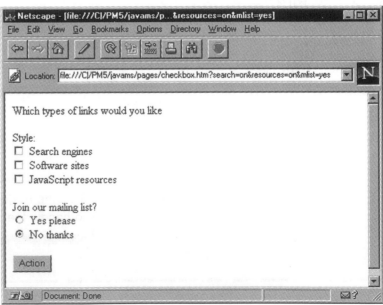

Links from lists

Drop-down lists created the **<SELECT>** and **<OPTION>** tags have two forms. One allows only one selection at a time; the other accepts multiple selections. They need to be handled in different ways.

Single selections

The key to reading these in JavaScript code is to use the **selectedIndex** property of the list. If you have set up a list in *form1* with:

```
<SELECT NAME = choice>
```

then this will give you the index (counting from 0 at the top of the list):

```
chosen = document.form1.choice.selectedIndex
```

You can then use the index value in a set of if... tests, to react to the selection, or – as in the example – use it to pick out an element from an array. Here, the array holds URLs and the function *setURL()* jumps to the selected site.

```
function setURL()
{
    chosen =document.form1.choice.selectedIndex
    jump = link[chosen]
    window.location = jump
}
```

You could, of course, achieve the same result by displaying a simple <UL> list of links and jump directly from one. The advantage of this approach is that a drop-down list takes up very little screen space.

select.htm

```
<HTML>
<HEAD>
<SCRIPT>
link = new Array(5)
    link[0] = "ftp://kth.se/pub/tex/tools/pkzip/pkz204g.exe"
    link[1] = "ftp://ftp.microsoft.com/"
    link[2] = "ftp:////ftp1.netscape.com/"
    link[3] = "ftp://micros.hensa.ac.uk/mirrors/cica/"
    link[4] = "ftp://oak.oakland.edu/pub/msdos"
```

Set up the array of links

```
function setURL()
{
    chosen =document.form1.choice.selectedIndex
    jump = link[chosen]
    window.location = jump
}

</SCRIPT>
</HEAD>
<BODY>
<H3>Useful FTP links</H3>
<FORM NAME = form1>
<SELECT NAME = choice>
<OPTION = pkzip>Download PKZIP (197Kb)
<OPTION = microsoft>Microsoft's ftp site
<OPTION = netscape>One of the Netscape ftp servers
<OPTION = ukmirror>The UK mirror of the great CICA archives
<OPTION = oak>The Oak Software Library
</SELECT>
<P>
<INPUT TYPE = button VALUE = "Go for it" onClick = "setURL()">
</FORM>
</BODY>
</HTML>
```

This is the NAME of the SELECT object – compare this with the equivalent line in the next example

The OPTIONs identifiers are not used by JavaScript

Take note

OPTIONs do not have an onClick event, though they do have onBlur, onFocus and onChange. You could link code to one of these.

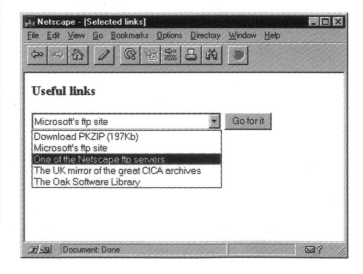

140

Multiple selections

If you write the **MULTIPLE** keyword into a **<SELECT>** tag, your visitors will be able to select more than one option (in the usual way – by holding down [Control] while clicking).

```
<SELECT MULTIPLE NAME = os>
```

The **selectIndex** of the whole **<SELECT>** set is then no longer of use. We now need to use the **selected** property (a *true* or *false* value) of the individual **<OPTION>**s. These form an array, the name of which comes from the **<SELECT>** tag, and can be conveniently tested in a loop:

```
for(loop = 0; loop <document.form1.os.length; loop++)
    if (document.form1.os[loop].selected)
```

● **document.form1.os.length** tells you the number of <OPTION>s in the set.

● **document.form1.os[loop].selected** returns the state of one <OPTION>.

One of the more useful properties of <OPTION>s is text. This is the text displayed in the drop-down list. If you want your visitors to confirm their selections, you can display this.

In the next example, visitors are asked to select the operating systems that interest them. When they click the 'Show selection' button, the *show( )* function will check through the array and add the text of selected options to the *temp* string, then copy the finished string into the TEXTAREA for display.

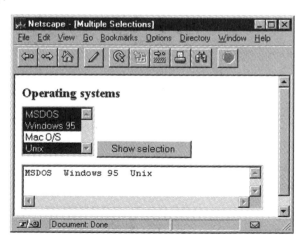

multsel.htm

```
<HTML>
<HEAD>
<TITLE>Multiple Selections</TITLE>
<SCRIPT>
function show()
{
    temp = ""
    for(loop = 0; loop < document.form1.os.length; loop++)
        if (document.form1.os[loop].selected)
            temp = temp + document.form1.os[loop].text + " "
    document.form1.showos.value = temp
}
</SCRIPT>
</HEAD>
<BODY>
<H3>Operating systems</H3>
<FORM NAME = form1>
<SELECT MULTIPLE NAME = os>
<OPTION = dos>MSDOS
<OPTION = win95>Windows 95
<OPTION = macos>Mac O/S
<OPTION = unix>Unix
</SELECT>

<INPUT TYPE = button VALUE = "Show selection"
onClick = "show()">
<P><TEXTAREA NAME = showos ROWS = 2 COLS = 40>
</TEXTAREA>
</FORM>
</BODY>
</HTML>
```

> length is 1 more than the index of the last element so use **<** test

> Add the display text to the string if the option is selected

> So this array is called **os**

Take note

If you want more details about any aspect of JavaScript, remember that the JavaScript Guide is available on-line. Just start from the Handbook in Netscape's Help menu.

Feedback on-line

The next example pulls together some aspects of using FORM options in JavaScript, gives immediate feedback to the user and also generates e-mail feedback to the page's author.

At Hot Wheels you can insure your skateboard on-line! The cost of the insurance is based on the value of the board, but varies with the region in which the skateboarder lives, and with the level of cover required. This information is entered into, or selected from options in the form. *region* is a drop-down list; *cover* is a set of Radio buttons. Both could have been done either way, as in both cases only one item is being selected from a set.

The basic formula is:

£10 + (value of board/100) * regional rate * cover level

The premium is worked out in the function *calculate( )*. Here are the crucial lines:

```
howmuch = eval("document.form1.InsVal.value")
```

eval() is necessary to convert the text into a numeric value.

```
for(loop = 0; loop < document.form1.cover.length; loop++)
    if (document.form1.cover[loop].checked)
```

Radio button sets do not have a **selectedIndex** property. To find out which one was selected, we have to test the **checked** property of each button in the array.

```
level = loop + 1
```

This gives cover levels of 1, 2 or 3 – a crude multiplier. If you were doing this properly, you would probably want to select the level from an array of values. This has been done with the regional rates.

```
where =document.form1.region.selectedIndex
cost = eval(10 + howmuch / 100 * rate[where] * level)
document.form1.quote.value = cost
```

Note the 'Purchase' button. This calls up the *confirmPurchase( )* function which runs a confirm dialog box before sending the e-mail with the command:

```
document.form1.submit()
```

submit( ) is the JavaScript equivalent of **<INPUT TYPE = Submit...>**.

143

feedback.htm

```
<HTML>
<HEAD>
<TITLE>Feedback</TITLE>
<SCRIPT>
rate = new Array(4)
rate[0] = 8
rate[1] = 4
rate[2] = 6
rate[3] = 12

function calculate()
{
    howmuch = eval("document.form1.InsVal.value")

    for(loop = 0; loop < document.form1.cover.length; loop++)
        if (document.form1.cover[loop].checked)
            level = loop + 1

    where =document.form1.region.selectedIndex

    cost = eval(10 + howmuch / 100 * rate[where] * level)
    document.form1.quote.value = cost
}
function confirmPurchase()
{
    if (confirm("Are you sure you wish to purchase insurance from us?"))
        document.form1.submit()
}
</SCRIPT>
</HEAD>

<BODY>
<H1 ALIGN=CENTER>HotWheels</H1>
<H2 ALIGN=CENTER>Skateboard Insurance Specialists</H2>
<FORM NAME = form1 METHOD = post
    ACTION = "mailto:sales@hotwheels.co.uk">

<P><B>Value of board:</B>
<INPUT TYPE = text NAME = InsVal SIZE = 10>
```

Callouts:
- Regional rates
- Get numeric value from text
- Find cover level
- Region
- A Submit button would not give them the chance to change their minds

```
<P>Region
<SELECT NAME = region>
<OPTION = london>London
<OPTION = southwest>South West
<OPTION = rest>Rest of England
<OPTION = wales>Wales
</SELECT>

<BR><INPUT TYPE = Radio NAME = cover>Third Party
<BR><INPUT TYPE = Radio NAME = cover>Third Party Fire and Theft
<BR><INPUT TYPE = Radio NAME = cover CHECKED>Comprehensive

<P><INPUT TYPE = "button" NAME = "calc" VALUE = "Get quote"
      onClick = "calculate()">
<P><B>Your Quotation:<B>
<INPUT TYPE = "text" NAME = "quote" SIZE = 10>
<P><INPUT TYPE = "button" NAME = "done" VALUE = "Purchase"
      onClick = "confirmPurchase()">
</FORM>
</BODY>
</HTML>
```

CHECKED sets the default

It doesn't take much work to give visitors the chance to change their minds before submitting a form

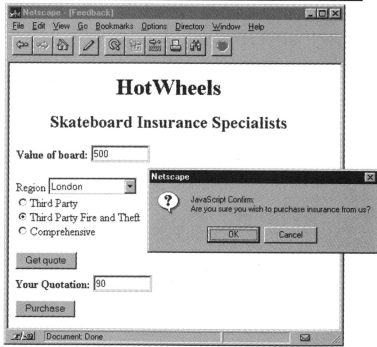

145

Checking entries

If a form is to be completed properly, some items of data may be essential – you must have the visitor's address if you are to send them something. Other entries may have to fall into a certain range of values – dates and order numbers must be valid.

Is there anything there?

You can easily check whether or not data has been entered into a text box, and with relatively little code, you can send your visitor back to enter something. Attach this to any text box or text area if you don't want your visitors to leave it blank:

```
onBlur = "if(this.value== '') {alert('Data please');this.focus()}"
```

this refers to whichever object it is attached to. If it is empty, the two following commands, held together in {brackets}, will be executed.

The **focus()** method places the cursor in a text box. (It also activates page, highlights buttons and selects other objects.)

this.focus() puts it into the current box. It works reliably when run from code within the event handler, though can get confused if used in functions. Somewhere in the process of transferring from page to function it can lose track of which **this** is which.

I like to keep event handling code as simple as possible, so in the next example, this kind of checking is managed by the function *checkData()*. The *elements[]* array number of the text box is passed to it, e.g.

```
onBlur = checkData(2)
```

The function then checks and responds as above.

```
function checkData(box)
{
    if(document.form1.elements[box].value == "")
    {
        alert("Please complete this box")
        document.form1.elements[box].focus()
    }
}
```

If you have several essential text boxes, this is a neater solution that attaching code directly to each.

Is it right?

Validation is another matter. Some things can be checked without too much trouble.

Is a number value in the right range?

```
checknum = eval(document.form.element[n].value)
if (checknum < 0 || checknum > 999)
    error routine...
```

Does the text box contains (unwanted) digits?

```
digits = false
for (loop = 0; loop < document.form.elements[n].value.length; loop++)
{
    c = document.form.elements[n].value.charAt(loop)
    if (c >= "0" && c <= "9")
        digits = true
}
if (digits)
    error routine...
```

The *validate()* function in the example checks an ISBN (book number). If you were doing this by hand, you would take each digit in turn, multiply the first by 1, the second by 2, and so on up to the last but one. The results are then added together and the total divided by 11. The remainder should be the same as the last digit.

For example, the ISBN of this book is 0 7506 3797 8. Do the sum:

$1*0 + 2*7 + 3*5 + 4*0 + 5*6 + 6*3 + 7*7 + 8*9 + 9*7 = 261/11 = 23$ r. 8

The routine works through the string, copying the number values into an array, and ignoring any spaces. If there aren't 10 digits, the code stops there and reports the error. The total is calculated and the modulus operator (%) used to find the remainder.

The notes on the program should help you to follow it in detail – but if you prefer, you could substitute a simple number range check instead and forget ISBNs!

```
<HTML>
<HEAD>
<TITLE>Validate</TITLE>
<SCRIPT>
function checkData(box)
{
    if(document.form1.elements[box].value == "")
    {
        alert("Please complete this box")
        document.form1.elements[box].focus()
    }
}

function validate()
{
num = new Array(10)
count = 0
total = 0
number = document.form1.isbn.value
for(loop = 0; loop < number.length; loop++)
{
    digit = number.charAt(loop)
    if(digit >= "0" && digit <= 9)
    {
        num[count] = eval(digit)
        count++
    }
    if (count == 10) break
}
if (count < 10)
    return false
for(loop = 0; loop < 9; loop++)
{
    total += num[loop] * (loop +1)
}
if((total % 11) == num[9])
    return true
else return false
}
</SCRIPT>
</HEAD>
```

elements[ ] subscript passed from **onBlur =**...

copy to a variable to make the next lines more readable

pick out the digits and convert to numbers

There must be 10 digits

Multiply and add to **total**

Compare remainder with last digit

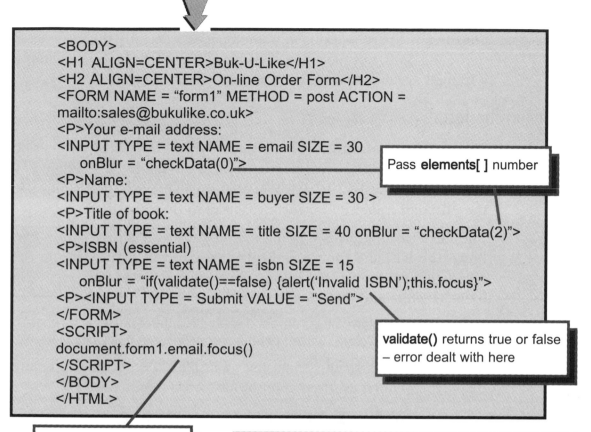

```
<BODY>
<H1 ALIGN=CENTER>Buk-U-Like</H1>
<H2 ALIGN=CENTER>On-line Order Form</H2>
<FORM NAME = "form1" METHOD = post ACTION =
mailto:sales@bukulike.co.uk>
<P>Your e-mail address:
<INPUT TYPE = text NAME = email SIZE = 30
    onBlur = "checkData(0)">
<P>Name:
<INPUT TYPE = text NAME = buyer SIZE = 30 >
<P>Title of book:
<INPUT TYPE = text NAME = title SIZE = 40 onBlur = "checkData(2)">
<P>ISBN (essential)
<INPUT TYPE = text NAME = isbn SIZE = 15
    onBlur = "if(validate()==false) {alert('Invalid ISBN');this.focus}">
<P><INPUT TYPE = Submit VALUE = "Send">
</FORM>
<SCRIPT>
document.form1.email.focus()
</SCRIPT>
</BODY>
</HTML>
```

Pass **elements[ ]** number

validate() returns true or false
– error dealt with here

Put cursor in the **email**
text box at the start

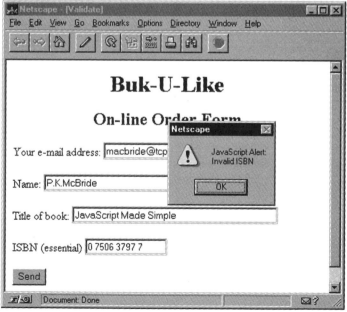

149

Working in frames

For the most part, working in framed pages is exactly the same as in unframed ones, but there are a few nice little touches you can add to a framed system using JavaScript. Here are just a couple.

Following the focus

The **onFocus** and **onBlur** events occur when the visitor enters and leaves a page. With simple pages, these are of limited use. When you have a framed system, where your visitor can move between pages in the different frames, it is worth reacting to these events.

The next example uses a two-frame layout, with a 'navigation bar' down the left, and the main display area to the right. Code in the navigation bar toggles the colours of the two areas so that the one in focus is white and the other is blue.

```
onBlur="document.bgColor= 'blue'; parent.display.document.bgColor = 'white' "
onFocus="document.bgColor= 'white'; parent.display.document.bgColor = 'blue' "
```

parent refers up to the enclosing **<FRAMESET>** document, where display is defined as the second frame.

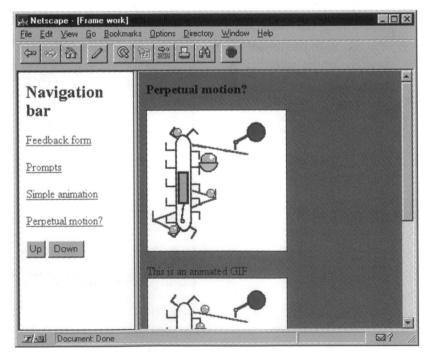

Because there are only two frames here, it is sufficient to have the colour-setting code in just one frame – if it isn't in focus, the other one must be. With three or more frames, the simplest approach is to write code into each document that changes its own colour only.

Remote control

The **scroll()** method will move a document in a window or frame, just as if you were using the standard Windows scrollbars. There is little advantage in implementing this on a simple page – it is easier to use the scrollbars. With a framed system there is an advantage – if you put your scroll controls in the navigation frame, along with the links, then your visitor can control the whole display from one place.

The method is used in the form:

document.scroll(*newX, newY*)

With the *newX* and *newY* values being measured in pixels (screen dots), counting from the top left corner of the page. They can be given as actual values, e.g.

document.scroll(0,500)

This would scroll the page up by roughly one screenful on an 800 x 640 display. The example on the next page uses a variable, *frametop*, and adjusts this by 200 in the *scrollup( )* and *scrolldown( )* functions.

To implement this example, type in and save the two documents, but replacing the links to existing pages of your own. At least one of these should be long enough to test out the scrolling routines!

topframe1.htm

```
<HTML>
<FRAMESET COLS = 30%,*>
<FRAME SRC = "navigate.htm" NAME = "navbar">
<FRAME SRC = "contents.htm" NAME = "display">
</FRAMESET>
</HTML>
```

Replace with the name of your opening display page

navigate.htm

```html
<HTML>
<HEAD>
<TITLE>Navigation bar</TITLE>
<SCRIPT>
frametop = 0

function scrollup()
{
    frametop = (frametop >= 200) ? frametop - 200 : 0
    parent.display.scroll(0,frametop)
}
function scrolldown()
{
    frametop = frametop + 200
    parent.display.scroll(0,frametop)
}
</SCRIPT>
</HEAD>

<BODY BGCOLOR= "white" onBlur= "document.bgColor= 'blue';
    parent.display.document.bgColor = 'white' "
  onFocus= "document.bgColor= 'white';
    parent.display.document.bgColor = 'blue' ">

<H2>Navigation bar</H2>
<A HREF = "feedbck1.htm" TARGET = "display">Feedback form</A>
<P>
<A HREF = "prompts.htm" TARGET = "display">Prompts</A>
<P>
<A HREF = "animate.htm" TARGET = "display">Simple animation</A>
<A HREF = "perp.htm" TARGET = "display">Perpetual motion?</A>
<FORM>
<INPUT TYPE = "button" VALUE = "Up" onClick = "scrollup()">
<INPUT TYPE = "button" VALUE = "Down" onClick = "scrolldown()">
</FORM>
</BODY>
</HTML>
```

Initialise **frametop** for the scrolling functions

Subtract 200 if possible – otherwise set to 0

Use the JavaScript colour names

Substitute your own pages here

Window control

As a general rule, if you need to open a new window to display a page, using the **TARGET = _blank** option in the **HREF** tag will do the job well enough. Sometimes it will be the best solution – and it will always be the simplest. However, there are times when you may like to have the extra control that you get by using JavaScript to open a window.

window.open()

The **open()** method lets you specify the size of the window and which frame components (scrollbars, title bar, menu bar, etc) to include. The basic shape is:

varname = **window.open**(*URL*, *winName*, *components*)

Virtually every bit of this method is optional!

- *varname* is needed if you want to run any methods or access any properties of the window.

- *URL* is used to load in a page.

- *winName* is only needed if the window will be used as a TARGET from code in another window.

- The *components* are **toolbar**, **location**, **directories**, **status**, **menubar**, **scrollbars**, **resizable** – all of which are set by *yes* or *no*. You only need to set the ones you want on – the rest will be off. **width** and **height** can also be set – in pixels. All of the settings are done in one string, separated by commas, and you **must not** put spaces around the '=' sign.

Some examples of its use:

window.open("http://www.yahoo.com")

Simply opens a standard browser window and loads in the page.

win2 = (" ", "NewWin", "width=300,height=400")

Opens an empty window, with no components, 300 by 400 pixels, giving it a TARGET name of *NewWin*, and a variable name of *win2*.

win2 = ("mini.htm", "", "toolbars=yes,width=300,height=500")

Opens a window, with a toolbar only, 300 by 500 pixels, and displays the *mini.htm* page.

Filling the window

When opened, the window can display an existing page file, or you can use the **write( )** method to define the contents at the time, varying them in response to some previous feedback from the visitor. It is possible – though hard work – to construct large and complex pages, entirely through **write( )**.

In this first example, a window is opened, not to display a page, but as a 'pop-up' which tells the visitor more about a link on the page. As you can see in the screenshot, pointing at a link opens the window – and pointing at **Close** in the pop-up window, closes it.

The opening code is all in the function *popup(),* which is called by the **onMouseOver** event of the links. This is the basic shape:

```
<A HREF = "http://www...page ref..."
    onMouseOver = "popup('text to display')">...Link text...</A>
```

When the mouse passes over the link, the event handler calls *popup()*, passing it a string of text.

popup( ) opens a small window then uses **write( )** to create the display. There are two lines. The first writes the text, embedded in <H4> tags.

```
win2.document.write ("<H4>" + words + "</H4>")
```

The second creates a link, complete with its HREF, display text and onMouseOver code.

```
win2.document.write("<A HREF = ' '
    onMouseOver = 'self.close()'>Close</A><P>")
```

Three points to notice here:

- The **HREF** points to nothing. It would give an error if you tried to click on it, but you will never get the chance – as soon as you point to the link, the window will close.

- **close( )** shuts a window – **self.close( )** shuts the window that holds the expression.

- The **<P>** at the end of the last **write()** is essential. If you miss it out, the text will not be sent to the screen.

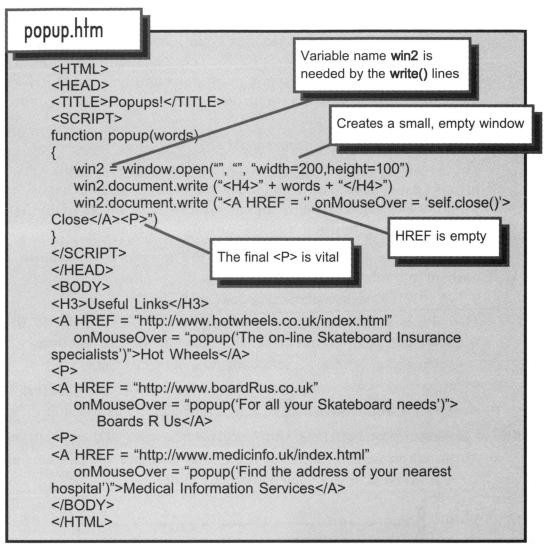

popup.htm

```
<HTML>
<HEAD>
<TITLE>Popups!</TITLE>
<SCRIPT>
function popup(words)
{
    win2 = window.open("", "", "width=200,height=100")
    win2.document.write ("<H4>" + words + "</H4>")
    win2.document.write ("<A HREF = '' onMouseOver = 'self.close()'>
Close</A><P>")
}
</SCRIPT>
</HEAD>
<BODY>
<H3>Useful Links</H3>
<A HREF = "http://www.hotwheels.co.uk/index.html"
    onMouseOver = "popup('The on-line Skateboard Insurance
specialists')">Hot Wheels</A>
<P>
<A HREF = "http://www.boardRus.co.uk"
    onMouseOver = "popup('For all your Skateboard needs')">
        Boards R Us</A>
<P>
<A HREF = "http://www.medicinfo.uk/index.html"
    onMouseOver = "popup('Find the address of your nearest
hospital')">Medical Information Services</A>
</BODY>
</HTML>
```

Variable name **win2** is needed by the **write()** lines

Creates a small, empty window

HREF is empty

The final <P> is vital

The catch to running onMouseOver on a link is that it will activate the code – whether you want it or not – when you try to click the link. In this case, you may have to move the pop-up window out of the way before you can click the link!

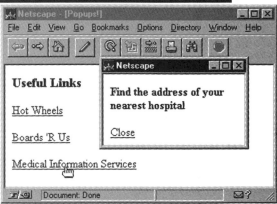

The javascript URL

Up to this point, all our JavaScript code has been run from event handlers or directly from a <SCRIPT>. There is another way. I have been ignoring it because it tends to produce untidy – and therefore hard to read – code. This approach revolves around the word '**javascript:**' used in a link.

<A HREF = "javascript:*command*">

The **javascript:...** fits into the place where you would normally see an **http://...** expression. The *command* doesn't have to be one that opens windows and loads up pages, but as visitors expect links to do that, it may be as well to use it mainly – or only – for that purpose.

In the example, the **javascript:** calls up the function *openWindow( )*, passing to it the URL of a page.

<A HREF = "javascript:openWindow('int31.htm')">

The URL is picked up by the parameter *winfile* and given to the **window.open** method that makes up the whole of this function.

window.open (winfile, '', 'scrollbars=no,width=280,height=370')

It would have been possible to open directly from the **javascript:** starter, but would have lead to this rather lengthy expression:

<A HREF = "javascript:window.open ('int31.htm', '', scrollbars=no,width=280,height=370')">

As the link also needs its display text and/or an image, plus the closing </A>, it would give you some very nasty code!

topframe3.htm

```
<HTML>
<HEAD>
<TITLE>Working with Windows - javascript</TITLE>
<SCRIPT>
function openWindow(winfile)
{
    window.open (winfile, '', 'scrollbars=no,width=280,height=370')
}
</SCRIPT>
</HEAD>
```

```
<BODY>
<H1 ALIGN=CENTER>A few more Made Simples</H1>
<A HREF = "javascript:openWindow('int31.htm')">
The Internet (for 3.1) <IMG SRC= "INT31.gif" HEIGHT=90 WIDTH=69>
</A>
<A HREF = "javascript:openWindow('int95.htm')">
The Internet (for 95) <IMG SRC= "INT95.gif" HEIGHT=90 WIDTH=69>
</A>
<P><A HREF = "javascript:openWindow ('win95.htm')">
Windows 95 <IMG SRC= "WIN95.gif" HEIGHT=90 WIDTH=69>
</A>
<A HREF = "javascript:openWindow ('off97.htm')">
Office 97 <IMG SRC= "OFF97.gif" HEIGHT=90 WIDTH=69>
</A>
</BODY>
</HTML>
```

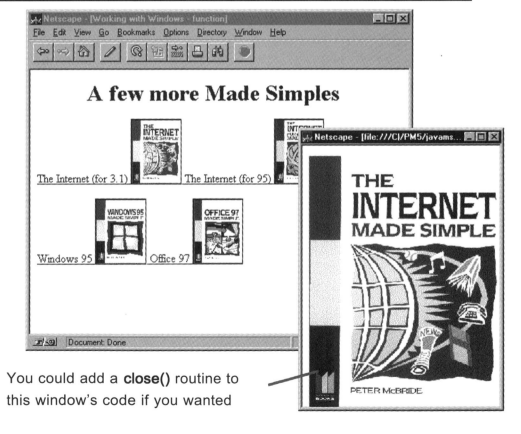

You could add a **close()** routine to this window's code if you wanted

Exercises

1   Create an on-line membership application form. It should ask for the applicant's name (an essential entry) and address, membership category (to be selected from at least 3 options) and the services required (with multiple selections allowed).

The document should contain a routine to calculate the membership cost on the basis of the category and services.

2   E-mail addresses are almost impossible to check properly – there is no single pattern – but you can make sure that they contain an '@' sign and at least one '.'. That should distinguish an e-mail address from a snail mail address, in case your visitor is confused.

Write a function that will return a false value if the address does not contain '@' and '.'.

9 JavaScript games

Problems and possibilities

JavaScript is a fully-fledged programming language, and capable of being used for more or less any kind of program, but it does have its limitations. The main one is that the output is relatively static. You can change the *contents* of a text box or an image, but you cannot change their *positions* – not without reloading the page.

The second limitation is size, or rather, downloading time. In theory, with one of the latest modems and a good Internet service provider, you should be able to download at 100Kb per second. In practice, you rarely reach a fraction of this speed – around 2Kb is more typical.

Random games

With the random number generator, you can roll dice, shuffle cards, select from lists, and generally make things happen unexpectedly. There are two examples of this type in this chapter: *Guess* is a simple number-guessing game; *Dice* lets you roll them bones against the computer.

Word games

The string methods have all you need to manipulate text in many ways, making word games an obvious area for JavaScript development. The trickiest bits here are often analysing the games beforehand, so that you can define exactly what happens at each stage. There's a full version of Hangman in this chapter – it even has a scaffold!

Grid games

Positional games, played on a grid of squares, can be implemented on screen through arrays of images or textboxes. As long as you stick to two (human) players, these are not usually too difficult to design – the real problems come when you try to write code to let the computer play a sensible game. Even something as simple as noughts and crosses takes quite a lot of work, as you can see on page 172.

Guess the number

This is an interactive version of the guessing game from Chapter 5. It is included, not as an example of a great game – once you've worked out the strategy, you can win every time – but to demonstrate the use of functions with parameters and return values.

The player types a number into the first text box (*guessbox*), then presses the *Check* button. This calls up the *checkit( )* function, which compares the guess with the target number and outputs an appropriate message through the second text box (*feedback*).

Look first at the Check button's **onClick** call:

"document.form1.feedback.value=checkit(document.form1.guessbox.value)"

This passes the *guessbox* value to *checkit( )*, and copies its return value into *feedback*. In *checkit( )*, the value is taken into the *guessText* parameter, and first checked to see if anything is there before using **eval( )** to turn it into a number. Trying to evaluate an empty string would create an error.

```
function checkit(guessText)
{
    if (guessText == "")
        return("Nothing entered")
    else
        ...
        guess = eval(guessText)
```

There are five possible exits from the function, with each returning a different message string.

Some graphics would improve the appearance, and using Timeout to set a time limit might add a little tension

```
<HTML>
<HEAD>
<TITLE>Guess</TITLE>
<SCRIPT>
function game()
{
    x = Math.round(Math.random()*100)
    count = 0
    document.form1.guessbox.value = ""
    document.form1.feedback.value = ""
}
function checkit(guessText)
{
    if (guessText == "")
        return("Nothing entered")
    else
    {
        count++
        if (count == 8)
            return("The number was " + x)
        guess = eval(guessText)
        if (guess > x)
            return("Too high")
        else if (guess < x)
            return("Too low")
        else return("You guessed it in " + count + " goes")
    }
}
</SCRIPT>
</HEAD>
<BODY>
<FORM NAME = form1>
Enter your guess:
<INPUT TYPE = text NAME = guessbox SIZE = 5>
<P><INPUT TYPE = button VALUE = " Check " onClick =
"document.form1.feedback.value=checkit(document.form1.guessbox.value)">
<P><INPUT TYPE = text NAME = feedback SIZE = 25>
<P><INPUT TYPE = button VALUE = " New game " onClick = "game()">
</FORM>
</BODY>
</HTML>
```

> Set the random number and the guess counter, and clear the text boxes

> Only allow 8 guesses – what would happen if you moved these lines to the end of the function?

162

Dice

This is just the bare bones (pardon the pun) of a dice game. You and the computer both roll three dice. The score is the total face value, with a bonus of 10 for a pair or 20 for three of a kind.

There are three things that I want you to focus on here: the use of the elements[] array, the use of a variable array for checking, and the logical tests.

The text boxes are accessed not by name, but through the *elements[]* array. This allows us to use one function for both players' goes.

```
function game(first)
```

When *first* is 0, this will roll the top set of dice (in *elements[0]* to *elements[2]*. When *first* is 4, it rolls the dice in *elements[4]* to *[6]*. When the player clicks the "Roll them bones" button, this calls the *game()* function twice, before calling *whowon()* to check the scores.

```
onClick = "game(0); game(4); whowon()">
```

The dice values are stored in the *x[]* array for checking. It would be possible to work from the values in the text boxes, but the code would look horrendous. Instead of referring to the first dice by a neat *x[0]*, you would have to write *document.form1.elements[0].value* – and likewise for the dozen other referrences to the dice!

The logical tests revolve around the **&&** (AND) and | | (OR) operators. You can only compare two values at a time with the == operator – unfortunately **x[0] == x[1] == x[2]** won't work!

There are three of a kind if the first and second are the same, **AND** the first and third are the same:

```
if (x[0] == x[1] && x[0] == x[2])
```

We have a pair if either the first and second, **OR** the first and third, **OR** the second and third are the same:

```
if (x[0] == x[1] || x[0] == x[2] || x[1] == x[2])
```

dice.htm

```
<HTML>
<HEAD>
<TITLE>Dice</TITLE>
<SCRIPT>
myscore = 0
yourscore = 0

function game(first)
{
    var x = new Array(3)
    for (loop = 0; loop <  3; loop++)
    {
        x[loop] = Math.ceil(Math.random() * 6)
        document.form1.elements[loop+first].value = x[loop]
    }
    score = x[0] + x[1] + x[2]
    if (x[0] == x[1] && x[0] == x[2])
        score += 20
    else if (x[0] == x[1] || x[0] == x[2] || x[1] == x[2])
        score += 10

    document.form1.elements[first+3].value = score

    if (first == 0)
        myscore = score
    else yourscore = score
}

function whowon()
{
    if (myscore > yourscore)
        document.form1.winner.value = "I win"
    else if (myscore < yourscore)
        document.form1.winner.value = "You win"
    else
        document.form1.winner.value = "Drawn game"
}
</SCRIPT>
</HEAD>
```

ceil() rounds *up* – this gives values between 1 and 6

The values go into elements 0, 1 and 2, or into 4, 5 and 6

Calculate the total, then test for bonuses

Storing the totals in myscore and yourscore makes it easier to test for the winner – the alternative is to test the values in the text

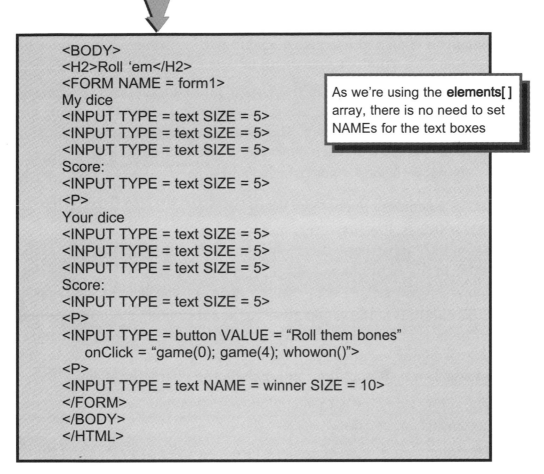

```
<BODY>
<H2>Roll 'em</H2>
<FORM NAME = form1>
My dice
<INPUT TYPE = text SIZE = 5>
<INPUT TYPE = text SIZE = 5>
<INPUT TYPE = text SIZE = 5>
Score:
<INPUT TYPE = text SIZE = 5>
<P>
Your dice
<INPUT TYPE = text SIZE = 5>
<INPUT TYPE = text SIZE = 5>
<INPUT TYPE = text SIZE = 5>
Score:
<INPUT TYPE = text SIZE = 5>
<P>
<INPUT TYPE = button VALUE = "Roll them bones"
    onClick = "game(0); game(4); whowon()">
<P>
<INPUT TYPE = text NAME = winner SIZE = 10>
</FORM>
</BODY>
</HTML>
```

As we're using the **elements[ ]** array, there is no need to set NAMEs for the text boxes

The game could be extended to have five dice, though the checking routine gets more complex with each extra dice

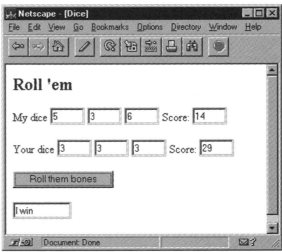

Hangman

Hangman is a good exercise in manipulating strings. It also gives us another opportunity to play with images.

The core of the game is in the *check( )* function. *letter* is the guess; *word* is the one to find; *show* starts full of asterisks, which are replaced by correct letters. The routine works through *word*, using **chartAt( )** to pick up each character in turn for checking.

```
for (loop= 0; loop < word.length; loop++)
{
    if (word.charAt(loop) == letter)
```

If it matches, the characters up to and after the match are sliced off *show* into substrings, then joined back together with the guessed letter in the right place.

```
show=show.substring(0,loop) + letter + show.substring(loop+1,word.length)
```

Look carefully at the values given to the **substring( )** method. The first is the index of the first character to include; the second is the index of the character *after* the last one that you want to include. So, **show.substring(0,loop)** does not include the character at *loop*.

The reformed *show* is then copied to the screen.

```
document.hangform.display.value = show
```

The found letter must be removed from *word* – so cheats can't boost their score by continually guessing the same correct letter. The substrings are cut from *word* and rejoined in exactly the same way.

```
word = word.substring(0,loop) + "*" + word.substring(loop+1,word.length)
```

hangman.htm

Create your own word set – use only upper case to make checking easier

```
<HTML>
<HEAD>
<SCRIPT>
wordArray = new Array("AARDVARK","BEE","CHEETAH","DINGO","ELK",
"FOX","GIRAFFE","HYENA","IBEX","JAGUAR","KOALA","LION",
"MONGOOSE","NEWT","OX","POSSUM","QUAGGA","REINDEER",
"SQUIRREL", "TIGER","UNICORN","VOLE","WALRUS","XIPHIAS","ZEBRA")
```

```
function loadImages()
{
    pic0 = new Image()
    pic0.src = "hang0.gif"
    pic1 = new Image()
    pic1.src = "hang1.gif"
    pic2 = new Image()
    pic2.src = "hang2.gif"
    pic3 = new Image()
    pic3.src = "hang3.gif"
    pic4 = new Image()
    pic4.src = "hang4.gif"
    pic5 = new Image()
    pic5.src = "hang5.gif"
    pic6 = new Image()
    pic6.src = "hang6.gif"
    pic7 = new Image()
    pic7.src = "hang7.gif"
    pic8 = new Image()
    pic8.src = "hang8.gif"
    pic9 = new Image()
    pic9.src = "hang9.gif"
    pic10 = new Image()
    pic10.src = "hang10.gif"
    picA = new Array(pic0,pic1,pic2,pic3,pic4,pic5,pic6,pic7,pic8,pic9,pic10)
}

function checkload()
{
    if (pic10.complete == false)
        setTimeout("checkload()",100)
}

function newgame()
{
    checkload()
    count = 0
    document.scaffold.src = pic0.src
    x = Math.ceil(Math.random() * 26)
    word = wordArray[x]
    wordcopy = word
    target = 0
```

> The image-handling routines are almost identical to those used in the simple animation in Chapter 7

> **checkload()** is only needed here on the first time, but later calls will take virtually no time

> random number 1 to 26

> Copy may be needed at end if player can't guess it

167

```
    show = ""
    for (loop = 0; loop <word.length; loop++)
        show += "*"
    document.hangform.display.value = show
    document.hangform.tried.value = ""
}
function nextpic()
{
    count++
    if (count <= 10)
        document.scaffold.src = picA[count].src
    else alert("You lose. The word was " + wordcopy)
}
function check(letter)
{
    letter =letter.charAt(0)
    letter = letter. toUpperCase()
    found = false
    for (loop= 0; loop < word.length; loop++)
    {
    if (word.charAt(loop) == letter)
        {
        show=show.substring(0,loop) + letter + show.substring(loop+1,word.length)
        document.hangform.display.value = show
        word=word.substring(0,loop) + "*" + word.substring(loop+1,word.length)
        found = true
        target++
        }
    }
    if (target == word.length)
        alert("You win")
    if (found == false)
    {
        nextpic()
        document.hangform.tried.value += letter
    }
    document.hangform.guess.value = ""
}
</SCRIPT>
```

Create a string of asterisks the same length as **word**

Display the next image, building the scaffold

Just in case – take the first letter only and force it to upper case

Good guess?

Add to 'bad guesses' string

Clear text box for next guess

```
<BODY>
<SCRIPT>
loadImages()
</SCRIPT>
<IMG NAME = scaffold SRC = hang0.gif WIDTH = 158 HEIGHT = 210>
<FORM NAME = hangform>
What's this word?
<INPUT TYPE = text NAME = display VALUE = "***********">
<P>Guess a letter
<INPUT TYPE = text NAME = guess SIZE = 2>
<P><INPUT TYPE = button VALUE = "Check the guess" onClick =
check(this.form.guess.value)>
<P>Bad Guesses
<INPUT TYPE = text NAME = tried VALUE = "" SIZE = 20>
<P><INPUT TYPE = button VALUE = "New game" onClick = "newgame()">
</FORM>
<SCRIPT>
newgame()
</SCRIPT>
</BODY>
</HTML>
```

Noughts and Crosses

It's only when you try to code so that the computer can play a game that you appreciate the skill that goes into chess programs. Even with a simple game like Noughts and Crosses, it takes quite a bit of thinking and over a page of code to get the computer to play moderately well.

Here's the thinking behind the code.

A player must be able to:

- recognise a win when there are 3 Xs or 3 Os in a line
- check for 2 Xs or 2 Os, so it can block you or fill a winning line
- know the best place to go when there is no obvious move.

We can tell all this by looking at the board. The 'board', in this case, is a set of text boxes, and the computer could check their contents, but that would mean checking every possible layout in each line, e.g. 2 Xs can be X – X, XX– or –XX. We can simplify things by mapping the board into an array and giving a number to the Xs and Os. If we make O worth 1 and X worth 4, then we can find the total for each line and just check that.

- 12 shows 3 Xs, which in this game means the human has won.
- 3 shows 3 Os, meaning that the computer has won.
- 8 means 2 Xs, and 2 means 2 Os. In either case, the computer should find the empty square and mark its O to block, or win.

Of course, we have to do this for every line – across, down and diagonal. Some parts of the coding would be simpler if the array was two-dimensional, but as the text boxes form into the one-dimensional *elements[]* array, it is simpler overall to stay in one dimension. The *board[]* array maps onto the text boxes like this:

0	1	2
3	4	5
6	7	8

Which leads us to this **for...** loop to check the rows:

```
for (row = 0; row < 7; row += 3)
```

row holds 0, then 3, and finally 6. Here's the full row-checking routine.

```
for (row = 0; row < 7; row += 3)
{
    total = board[row] + board[row+1] + board[row+2]
    if (total == 12)
        return("You win")
    if (total == 3)
        return("I win")
}
for (row = 0; row < 7; row += 3)
{
    total = board[row] + board[row+1] + board[row+2]
    if (total == 8 || total == 2)
        for (col = 0; col < 3; col++)
            if (fill(row+col))
                return("Go again")
}
```

The repetition is unavoidable. We have to loop through the rows and columns twice – once to check for a winning line, and once to check for two of a kind. If we try to do all the checks in one loop, it would be possible to find two of a kind and miss a later winning line.

You will see that there are three possible exits from this, and the **returns** don't just force an exit, they also carry back a message. In all, there are 14 **returns** in *mymove( )*.

The *fill( )* function takes the number of a square, and – if it is empty – puts 'O' on the screen and 1 in the board[ ] array. It returns true if it made a move – notice how the last line of the row-checking routine tests *fill( )* as it calls it.

```
function fill(square)
{
    if (board[square]== 0)
    {
        board[square] = 1;
        document.form1.elements[square].value = "O"
        return true
    }
    return false
}
```

If there are no winning or two of a kind lines, what's the best move? You could get into some fairly hairy programming trying to work out the strategy, but you can let the computer play a reasonable game by rating the squares by how many lines cross through them. The centre square is the best (4 lines), followed by the corners (3 lines), then the centre-sides. The *bestmove[]* array lists their priority:

```
bestmove = new Array(4,0,2,6,8,1,3,5,7)
```

Compare the order of these numbers with the layout of the *board[]* .

The final lines of *mymove( )* run through this array, trying to fill each of the *bestmove* squares in turn.

```
for (loop= 0; loop< 9 ; loop++)
    if (fill(bestmove[loop])) return("Go again")
```

crosses.htm

```
<HTML>
<HEAD>
<TITLE>OXO</TITLE>
<SCRIPT>
function newgame()
{
    board = new Array(9)
    for (loop = 0; loop < 9; loop++)
    {
        document.form1.elements[loop].value = ""
        board[loop] = 0
    }
    bestmove = new Array(4,0,2,6,8,1,3,5,7)
}
function fill(square)
{
    if (board[square]== 0)
    {
        board[square] = 1;
        document.form1.elements[square].value = "O"
        return true
    }
    return false
}
```

> Create the **board[ ]** array, and clear it and the **elements[ ]**

> Create the **bestmove[ ]** array and initialise it

> If the square is empty, make your move

> Success...
> ... or failure

```
function mymove()
{
    for (square = 0; square < 9 ; square++)
        if (document.form1.elements[square].value== "X")
            board[square] = 4

    for (row = 0; row < 7; row += 3)
    {
        total = board[row] + board[row+1] + board[row+2]
        if (total == 12)
            return("You win")
        if (total == 3)
            return("I win")
    }
    for (row = 0; row < 7; row += 3)
    {
        total = board[row] + board[row+1] + board[row+2]
        if (total == 8 || total == 2)
            for (col = 0; col < 3; col++)
                if (fill(row+col))
                    return("Go again")
    }

    for (col = 0; col < 3; col++)
    {
        total = board[col] + board[col+3] + board[col+6]
        if (total == 12)
            return("You win")
        if (total == 3)
            return("I win")
    }
    for (col = 0; col < 3; col++)
    {
        total = board[col] + board[col+3] + board[col+6]
        if (total == 8 || total == 2)
            for (row = 0; row < 7; row += 3)
                if (fill(row+col))
                    return("Go again")
    }
```

Record all Xs in the **board[ ]** array

Check across the rows

3 Xs or 3 Os

2 Xs or 2 Os – find and fill the empty square

Check down the columns

Follow same checking routine for columns

```
                total = board[0] + board[4] + board[8]                    Check the diagonals
                if (total == 12)
                    return("You win")
                if (total == 3)                                  Check first for winning rows,
                    return("I win")                              then for two of a kind
                if (total == 8 || total == 2)
                    for (square = 0; square < 9; square += 4)
                        if (fill(square))
                            return("Go again")

                total = board[2] + board[4] + board[6]
                if (total == 12)
                    return("You win")
                if (total == 3)
                    return("I win")
                if (total == 8 || total == 2)
                    for (square = 0; square < 7; square += 2)
                        if (fill(square))
                            return("Go again")

                for (square = 0; square < 9 ; square++)          Find first empty square
                    if (fill(bestmove[square]))                  in bestmove[ ] array
                        return("Go again")

                return("No move")
            }
            </SCRIPT>                                  Should never reach here but JavaScript
            </HEAD>                                    gives an error if the function does not have
                                                       at least one unconditional return
            <BODY>
            <H2>Nought and Crosses</H2>
            <FORM NAME = form1>
            <INPUT TYPE = text SIZE = 2>
            <INPUT TYPE = text SIZE = 2>
            <INPUT TYPE = text SIZE = 2>
            <BR>
            <INPUT TYPE = text SIZE = 2>
            <INPUT TYPE = text SIZE = 2>
            <INPUT TYPE = text SIZE = 2>
```

```
<BR>
<INPUT TYPE = text SIZE = 2>
<INPUT TYPE = text SIZE = 2>
<INPUT TYPE = text SIZE = 2>
<P>
You play X, I'll play O
<SCRIPT>
newgame()
</SCRIPT>
<P><INPUT TYPE = button VALUE = " Check and move "
      onClick = "document.form1.feedback.value = mymove()">
<P><INPUT TYPE = button VALUE = "New game" onClick = "newgame()">
<P><INPUT TYPE = text NAME = feedback SIZE = 10>
</FORM>
</BODY>
</HTML>
```

Computer's move – display the return string in the **feedback** text box

This program can be beaten!

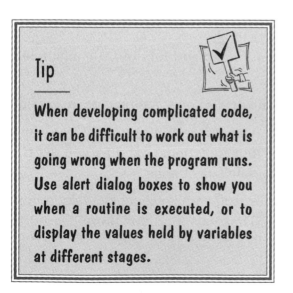

Tip

When developing complicated code, it can be difficult to work out what is going wrong when the program runs. Use alert dialog boxes to show you when a routine is executed, or to display the values held by variables at different stages.

Exercises

1   Go surfing and see what you can find in JavaScript. Here are some places you might like to start.

Yahoo's JavaScript links

http://www.yahoo.com/

Work through the menus: Computers and Internet > Programming Languages > JavaScript

HotSyte

http://www.serve.com/hotsyte

Good selection of resources and examples, with discussions and tutorials.

Java Script World

http://www.jsworld.com

Editorial plus loads of example scripts.

Live Software's JavaScript Resource Center

http://www.livesoftware.com

Well developed applications for the more advanced programmer.

The JavaScript Source!

http://www.compfund.com/javascript.main.html

A huge library of JavaScript code for you to cut and paste from.

Javascript: Simple Little Things To Add To Your Pages

http://www.tanega.com/java/java.htm

An enthusiast's page, full of useful links and lots of little examples. Fun! Well worth a visit.

2   Dip into the newsgroups. The main one is **news://comp.lang.javascript**.

Check out the FAQ (Frequently Asked Questions) lists. If you can't find what you want there, post your questions – and as you get the hang of things, reply to other people's problems.

Live Software host two groups: **livesoftware.javascript.developer** and **livesoftware.javascript.examples**. These are perhaps more geared to the professional, but you might like to give them a try.

176

10 Solutions to exercises

Chapter 1

Exercise 2

If you hit problems with this, check your punctuation! Have you closed your <tags> properly? Have you enclosed the status text in 'single quotes' and the whole onClick instruction in "double quotes"?

```
<HTML>
<HEAD>
<TITLE>Buttons</TITLE>
</HEAD>
<BODY>
<FORM>
<INPUT TYPE = button VALUE = " Coming?"
    onClick = "self.status = 'Welcome to my page' ">
<INPUT TYPE = button VALUE = " Going?"
        onClick = "self.status = 'Thanks for dropping by' ">
</FORM>
</BODY>
</HTML>
```

Chapter 2

Exercise 1

There are many possible solutions here. This is just one.

```
<HTML>
<TITLE> Feedback Form</TITLE>
<BODY>
<FORM METHOD = Post ACTION = mailto:macbride@tcp.co.uk>
<P>What did you think of my site?
<P>E-mail name: <INPUT TYPE = text NAME = email SIZE = 30>
<P>Real name: <INPUT TYPE = text NAME = realname SIZE = 30>
<P>How do you rate the site?

<BR><SELECT NAME = Platform>
<OPTION = great > Great!
<OPTION = fantastic> Fantastic!!
<OPTION = amazing> Amazing!!!
</SELECT>

<P>Any other comments?
<BR><TEXTAREA NAME = comments ROWS = 4 COLS = 40>
</TEXTAREA>

<P><INPUT TYPE = Submit VALUE = "Send the Form">
<INPUT TYPE = Reset VALUE = "Clear the Form">
</FORM>
</HTML>
```

If you want to get the right answers, you have got to ask the right questions!

Exercise 2

The page shouldn't be any more complicated than this. Make sure that your <A...> </A> tags are enclosed by the <LI> </LI> tags.

```
<HTML>
<HEAD>
  <TITLE>Links</TITLE>
</HEAD>
<BODY>
<H2>Places to go</H2>
<UL>
<LI><A HREF = "myhome.htm">Home page</A></LI>
<LI><A HREF = "form3.htm">Simple form</A></LI>
<LI><A HREF = "buttons.htm">Button demo</A></LI>
```

179

```
<LI><A HREF = "feedback.htm">Feedback form</A></LI>
</UL>
</BODY>
</HTML>
```

Exercise 3

Set the COLS option in <FRAMESET>, allowing 25 – 30% for the left-hand frame. The right-hand frame will need a name so that pages can be targeted into it.

```
<HTML>
<HEAD>
<TITLE>Framed system</TITLE>
</HEAD>
<FRAMESET COLS = 30%,*>
<FRAME SRC = "linklist.htm">
<FRAME SRC = "myhome.htm" NAME = "display">
</FRAMESET>
</HTML>
```

Add 'TARGET = framename' , 'TARGET = _top' or 'TARGET = _blank' as appropriate to open pages in the frame, the window or a new window.

```
<HTML>
<HEAD>
  <TITLE>Links</TITLE>
</HEAD>
<BODY>
<H2>Places to go</H2>
<UL>
<LI><A HREF = "index.htm" TARGET = display>Home page</A></LI>
<LI><A HREF = "form3.htm" TARGET = display>Simple form</A></LI>
<LI><A HREF = "buttons.htm" TARGET = _top>Button demo</A></LI>
<LI><A HREF = "feedback.htm" TARGET = _blank>Feedback form</A></LI>
</UL>
</BODY>
</HTML>
```

Chapter 3

Exercise 1

If you have problems getting this to work, double check the brackets and quotes, especially at the ends of line – they are easy to omit!

```
<HTML>
<HEAD>
<TITLE>Written pages</TITLE>
<SCRIPT>
document.write("<H1>Written from JavaScript</H1>")
document.write("<H3>or can you say 'JavaScripted'?</H3>")
document.write("This page was output from a Script")
document.write("<HR WIDTH = 50% NOSHADE>")
document.write("A bit more text")
document.write("<P>And another line...")
document.write("<BR>...or two")
</SCRIPT>
</HEAD>
<BODY>
</BODY>
<HTML>
```

Exercise 2

```
<HTML>
<HEAD>
<TITLE>Hidden</TITLE>
</HEAD>
<BODY BGCOLOR = "white" TEXT = "white">
<H2>Hidden Treasures</H2>
These pages are only to be read by those in the know.
<BR>We can't have just anybody reading them!
<FORM>
<INPUT TYPE = button VALUE = " Show me " onClick = "pass =
prompt('Enter the password', ''); document.bgColor = 'black'">
</FORM>
</BODY>
</HTML>
```

If you want to check the password, insert **if (pass == 'letmein')** – or whatever your password is – before **document.bgColor = 'black'**. As visitors can read your source code, this is not secure!

The if structure is covered in Chapter 5.

Chapter 4

Exercise 1

The worst thing about working with the values in text boxes is the length of their names. Once you have written the first, cut and paste to create the others – it doesn't just save typing time, it also saves typing errors!

```
<HTML>
<HEAD>
<TITLE>The Adder</TITLE>
</HEAD>
<BODY>
<FORM name = addform>
Enter numbers here
<INPUT TYPE = text NAME = number SIZE = 10>
<P>The total is:
<INPUT TYPE = text NAME = total VALUE = 0 SIZE = 10>
<P><INPUT TYPE = button VALUE = " Add to total " onClick =
"document.addform.total.value = eval(document.addform.total.value) +
eval(document.addform.number.value)")
</FORM>
</BODY>
</HTML>
```

Exercise 2

Get ready to cut and paste with this one – the **onClick()** expressions are awful! A minor problem here is getting the buttons to look good. Words would be clear, but symbols look better, except that a single character gives a tiny button. My solution has been to enclose the symbol in [+] brackets.

```
<HTML>
<HEAD>
<TITLE>Calculator?</TITLE>
</HEAD>
<BODY>
<FORM name = addform>
Enter numbers here
<INPUT TYPE = text NAME = number1 SIZE = 10>
<INPUT TYPE = text NAME = number2 SIZE = 10>
```

```
<P><INPUT TYPE = button VALUE = "[ + ]" onClick =
"document.addform.total.value = eval(document.addform.number1.value) +
eval(document.addform.number2.value)")>
<INPUT TYPE = button VALUE = "[ - ]" onClick =
"document.addform.total.value = eval(document.addform.number1.value) -
eval(document.addform.number2.value)")>
<INPUT TYPE = button VALUE = "[ * ]" onClick =
"document.addform.total.value = eval(document.addform.number1.value) *
eval(document.addform.number2.value)")>
<INPUT TYPE = button VALUE = "[ / ]" onClick =
"document.addform.total.value = eval(document.addform.number1.value) /
eval(document.addform.number2.value)")>
<P>The result is:
<INPUT TYPE = text NAME = total VALUE = 0 SIZE = 10>
</FORM>
</BODY>
</HTML>
```

Exercise 3

You just need to add these lines before the sort lines:

```
document.write("<H3>Reversed before sorting</H3>")
language.reverse()
for (n = 0; n < 8 ; n++)
    document.write("<BR>" + language[n]+ " Made Simple")
```

And the same again (with an edited heading!) afterwards.

Exercise 4

```
<HTML>
<BODY>
<SCRIPT>
visitor = prompt("Who is that?", "Your name?")
visitor.toUpperCase()
document.write("<H1>A big hello to " + visitor + "</H1>")
</SCRIPT>
The rest of the page follows here...
</BODY>
</HTML>
```

Chapter 5

Exercise 1

Using the rows value as the end test for the stars loop gives us one more asterisk in every line. After writing the asterisks, we must start a new line with a <BR>.

```
<HTML>
<BODY>
<SCRIPT>
for (rows = 1; rows <= 10; rows++)
{
    for (stars = 0; stars < rows; stars++)
        document.write("*")
    document.write("<BR>")
}
</SCRIPT>
</BODY>
</HTML>
```

Exercise 2

You must put either empty {} brackets or a semicolon after the **for...** line or the script will write "Done" every time round the loop.

```
<HTML>
<BODY>
<SCRIPT>
document.write("Starting to count<BR>")
for (loop = 1; loop <= 100000; loop++)
    {}
document.write("<BR>Done")
</SCRIPT>
</BODY>
</HTML>
```

Exercise 3

If the numbers are truly random, you would expect each value to occur almost – but not exactly – as often as each other. The totals should not vary be more than a few per cent, and the more numbers you generate, the smaller the variation should be.

```
<HTML>
<BODY>
<SCRIPT>
num = new Array(10)
document.write("Generating 10,000 random numbers<P>")
for (loop = 1; loop <= 10000; loop++)
{
    x = Math.floor(Math.random()*10)
    num[x]++
}
for (loop = 0; loop < 10; loop++)
document.write("<BR>Number " + loop + " frequency " + num[loop])
</SCRIPT>
</BODY>
</HTML>
```

Exercise 4

A for loop, running from the entered value down to 1, provides the simplest structure. All we need to do is multiply a temporary value – that starts as 1 – by the loop number.

```
<HTML>
<HEAD>
<SCRIPT>
function factorial(n)
{
    ans = 1
    for (loop = n; loop > 1; loop--)
        ans *= loop
    return ans
}
</SCRIPT>
</HEAD>
<BODY>
<SCRIPT>
number = prompt("Enter a number", "")
alert("Factorial " + number + " = " + factorial(number))
</SCRIPT>
</BODY>
</HTML>
```

Chapter 6

Exercise 1

Date values are held in milliseconds, so once we have got the difference between now and the date of the page, it has to be divided by 1000, then by 60, 60 and 24 to reduce it to days.

```
<HTML>
<HEAD>
<SCRIPT>
function doage()
{
    origin = new Date("August 12, 1997")
    now = new Date()
    elapsed = (now - origin)/1000        //seconds
    elapsed /= (60 *60 * 24)             //days
    document.dateform.age.value = Math.round(elapsed)
}
</SCRIPT>
</HEAD>
<BODY>
<FORM NAME = dateform>
<P>This page was last updated 12th August 1997
<INPUT TYPE = text NAME = age VALUE = "" SIZE = 4> days ago.
</FORM>
<SCRIPT>
doage()
</SCRIPT>
</BODY>
</HTML>
```

Exercise 2

If you just want to display seconds, the crucial line is simply:

```
document.timeform.stay.value = ((secs<10) ? ":0" : ":") + secs
```

If you want to display minutes as well, you must first find the (whole) number of minutes. Divide *secs* by 60, and round down with **floor()**.

```
m = Math.floor(secs/60)
```

Then multiply the minutes value by 60 and subtract that from the secs to find how many seconds remain:

```
s = secs - m * 60
```

```
<HTML>
<HEAD>
<SCRIPT>
function elapsed()
{
    m = Math.floor(secs/60)
    s = secs - m * 60
    document.form.stay.value = ((m<10) ? "0" : "") + m + ((s<10) ? ":0" : ":") + s
    secs++
    setTimeout("elapsed()",1000)
}
</SCRIPT>
</HEAD>
<BODY>
<FORM NAME = form1>
You have been here:
<INPUT TYPE = text NAME = stay VALUE = "" SIZE = 10>
</FORM>
<SCRIPT>
secs = 58
elapsed()
</SCRIPT>
</BODY>
</HTML>
```

Exercise 3

This is just a matter of copying the elapsed time function and its FORM text from exercise 2 and pasting it into the time of arrival page.

Exercise 4

The scrolling routine used here is the same as *setstatus()* on page 111. It is controlled through *scroll()* which checks the *going* value and sets or clears the Timeout accordingly, and flips going between true and false so the function can react to the next button click.

```
<HTML>
<HEAD>
<SCRIPT>
going = false
phrase = new String("Made Simples are good for you...Buy one now...")
```

```
function scrollon()
{
    len = phrase.length
    first = phrase.substring(0,1)
    rest = phrase.substring(1,len)
    phrase = rest + first
    self.status = phrase
    document.form1.display.value = phrase
    timerID = setTimeout("scrollon()",100)
}

function scroll()
{
    if (going)
    {
        clearTimeout(timerID)
        going = false
    }
    else
    {
        going = true
        scrollon()
    }
}
</SCRIPT>
</HEAD>
<BODY>
<FORM NAME = form1>
<INPUT TYPE = text NAME = display VALUE = "" SIZE = 40>
<P>
<INPUT TYPE = button VALUE = "Start/Stop" onClick = "scroll()">
</FORM>
</BODY>
</HTML>
```

Chapter 7

Exercise 1

Movement is much easier to manage when there is only one image to change. Here *red.gif* is replaced by the blank image, then the next image in the set is loaded with *red.gif*. When it reaches the end of the line, the place variable is reset to the start. The rest of the program follows the animate pattern from page 125.

```
<HTML>
<HEAD>
<SCRIPT>
timer = null
going = false
place = 0

function loadImages()
{
    pic0 = new Image()
    pic0.src = "red.gif"
    pic1 = new Image()
    pic1.src = "blank.gif"
}

function animate()
{
    if (going)
        clearTimeout(timer)
    document.images[place].src = pic1.src
    place++
    if (place > 7)                       // how many images do you have?
        place = 0
    document.images[place].src = pic0.src
    if (going)
        timer = setTimeout("animate()",100)
}
</SCRIPT>
</HEAD>
```

```
<BODY>
<SCRIPT>
loadImages()
</SCRIPT>
<IMG SRC= "red.gif">
<IMG SRC= "blank.gif">
<IMG SRC= "blank.gif">
<IMG SRC= "blank.gif">
<IMG SRC= "blank.gif">
<IMG SRC= "blank.gif">
<IMG SRC= "blank.gif">
<IMG SRC= "blank.gif">
<FORM>
<INPUT TYPE = "button" VALUE = "Start" onClick = "going = true;
animate()">
<INPUT TYPE = "button" VALUE = "Stop" onClick = "going = false;
animate()">
</FORM>
</BODY>
</HTML>
```

Exercise 2

All that's needed here is to use a variable for the delay, initally set to 100 or so, in the setTimeout().

```
timer = setTimeout("animate()",delay)
```
The faster and slower code can be attached directly to buttons. Slowing down is easily managed:

```
<INPUT TYPE = button VALUE = " Slower "
    onClick = "delay = delay + 10 ">
```
Speeding up requires a little extra code to prevent the delay from dropping below 0. Use of the condition ? : operator gives the neatest solution.

```
<INPUT TYPE = button VALUE = " Faster "
    onClick = "delay = delay - ((delay > 10) ? 10: 0)">
```

Chapter 8

Exercise 1

What your club does, is entirely up to you. Mine is for people addicted to the World Wide Web!

Here the e-mail entry check is attached directly to the event handler, as this is the only text box which is being checked.

```
<HTML>
<HEAD>
<SCRIPT>
membertype = new Array(10,25,15)
level = new Array(5,20,50,10)
function showcost()
{
    for(loop = 0; loop < 3; loop++)
        if(document.form1.category[loop].checked)
            fee = eval(membertype[loop])
    for(loop = 0; loop < 4; loop++)
        if(document.form1.services[loop].selected)
            fee += eval(level[loop])
    document.form1.cost.value = fee
}
</SCRIPT>
</HEAD>


<BODY>
<H1 ALIGN=CENTER>Web Watchers</H1>
<H2 ALIGN=CENTER>Membership Application Form</H2>
<FORM NAME = "form1" METHOD = post ACTION =
mailto:admin@webwatch.co.uk>
<P>Name: <INPUT TYPE = text NAME = user SIZE = 30
    onBlur = "if (this.value == '')
        {alert('Please enter your name'); this.focus()}">
<P>Address: <INPUT TYPE = text NAME = address SIZE = 30 >

<P>Membership category:
<BR><INPUT TYPE = Radio NAME = category>Junior (<18)
<BR><INPUT TYPE = Radio NAME = category>Adult
<BR><INPUT TYPE = Radio NAME = category>Senior/Unwaged
```

```
<P>Services required:
<SELECT MULTIPLE NAME = services>
<OPTION = breakit>Break addiction
<OPTION = cutit>Reduce dependence
<OPTION = feedit>Cheaper access
<OPTION = talkit>Meet other addicts
</SELECT>

<P><INPUT TYPE = button VALUE = "Show cost" onClick = "showcost()">
<P><INPUT TYPE = text NAME = cost SIZE = 10>
<P><INPUT TYPE = Submit VALUE = "Submit form">
<P><INPUT TYPE = Reset VALUE = "Clear and restart">
</FORM>

<SCRIPT>
document.form1.user.focus()
</SCRIPT>

</BODY>
</HTML>
```

Exercise 2

It is simplest to check for the two characters in two distinct routines. This checks first for an '@' sign, and exits at that point if none is found. It then runs an almost identical check for '.'.

Notice that a false value only generates an alert, and does not keep the visitor in the box – there are a few totally non-standard addresses!

```
<HTML>
<HEAD>
<SCRIPT>
function validmail()
{
    valid = false
    mail = document.form1.email.value
    for(loop = 0; loop < mail.length; loop++)
        if(mail.charAt(loop) == "@")
            valid = true
    if (valid == false)
        return false
    valid = false
```

```
      for(loop = 0; loop < mail.length; loop++)
          if(mail.charAt(loop) == ".")
                valid = true
      return valid
}
</SCRIPT>
</HEAD>
<BODY>
<FORM NAME = "form1">
<P>Your e-mail address:
<INPUT TYPE = text NAME = email SIZE = 30
    onBlur = "if(validmail()== false) alert('Please check your e-mail
address')">
</FORM>
</BODY>
</HTML>
```

Index